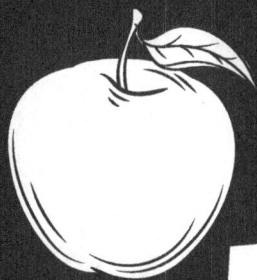

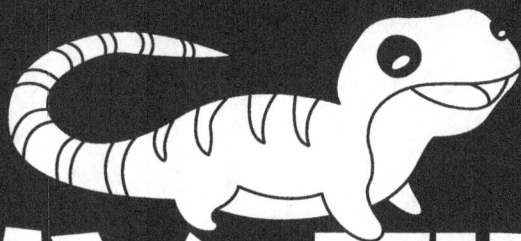

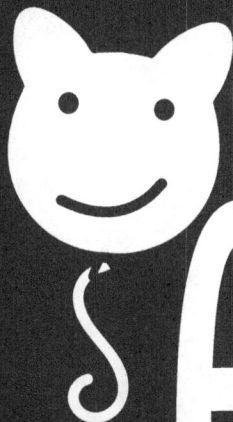

MY FIRST A-Z BOOK

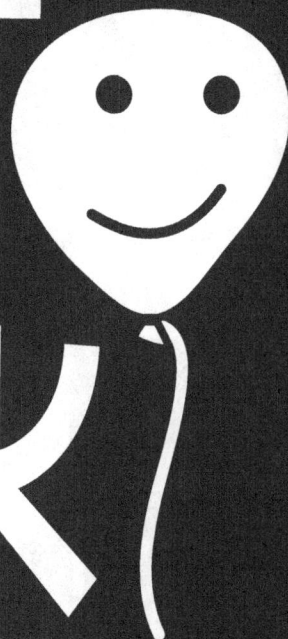

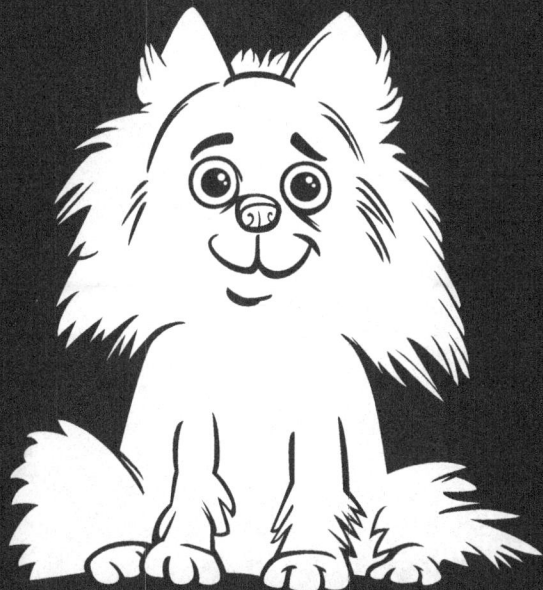

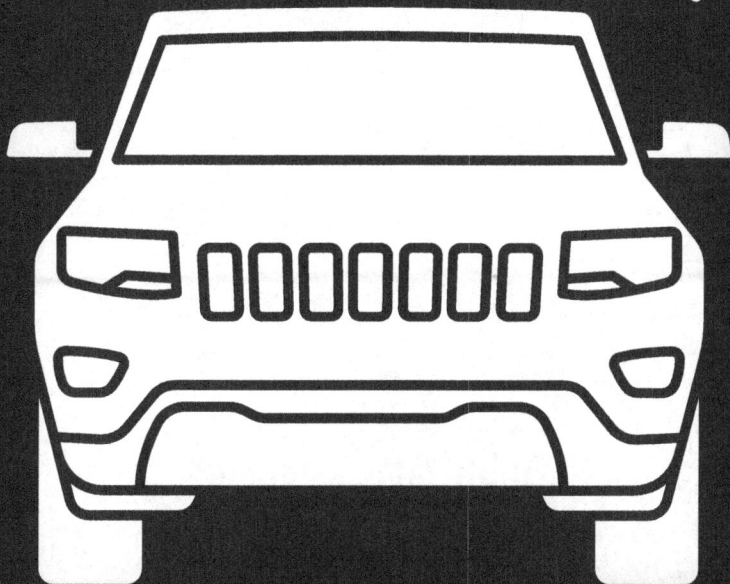

BABY NAME

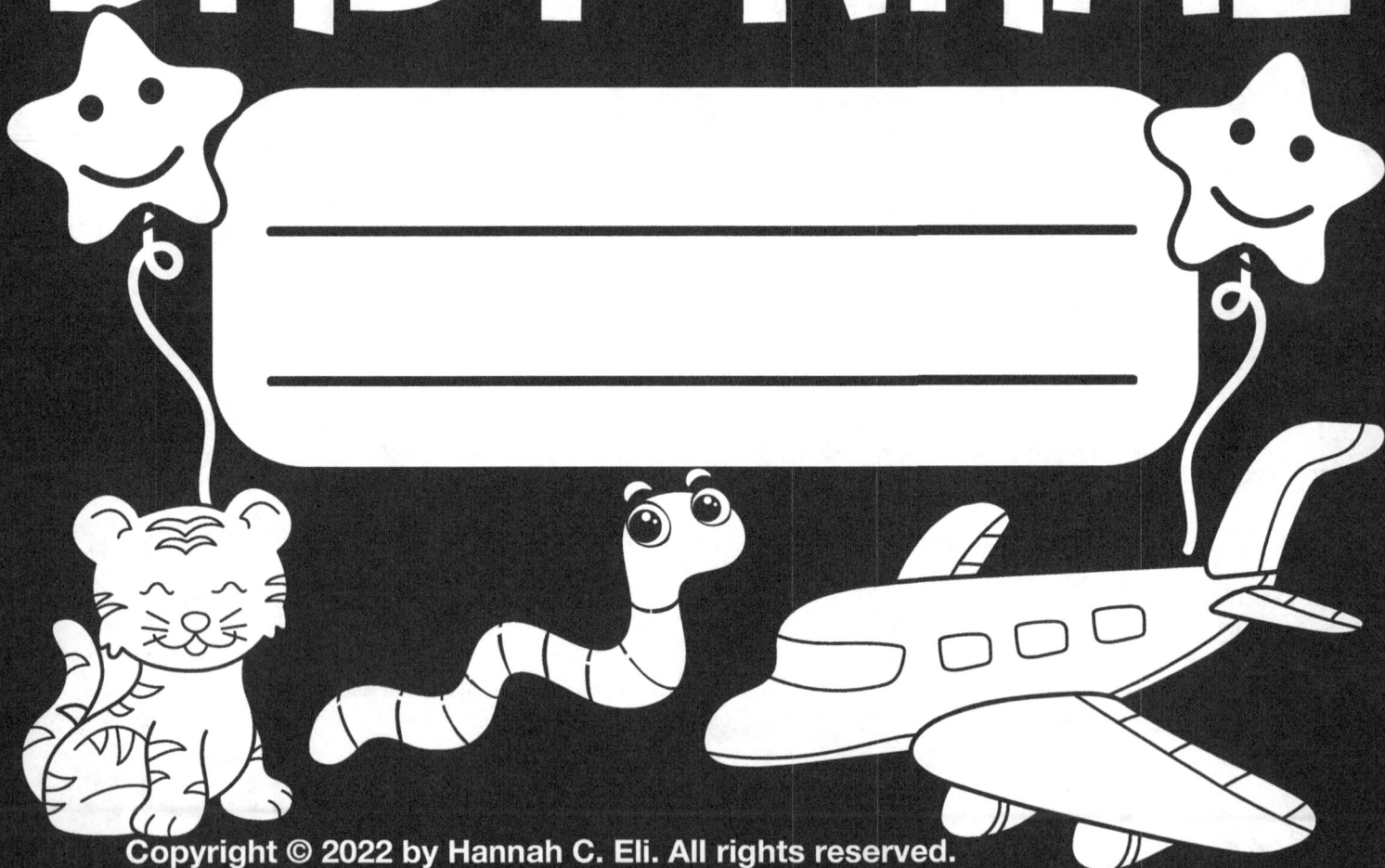

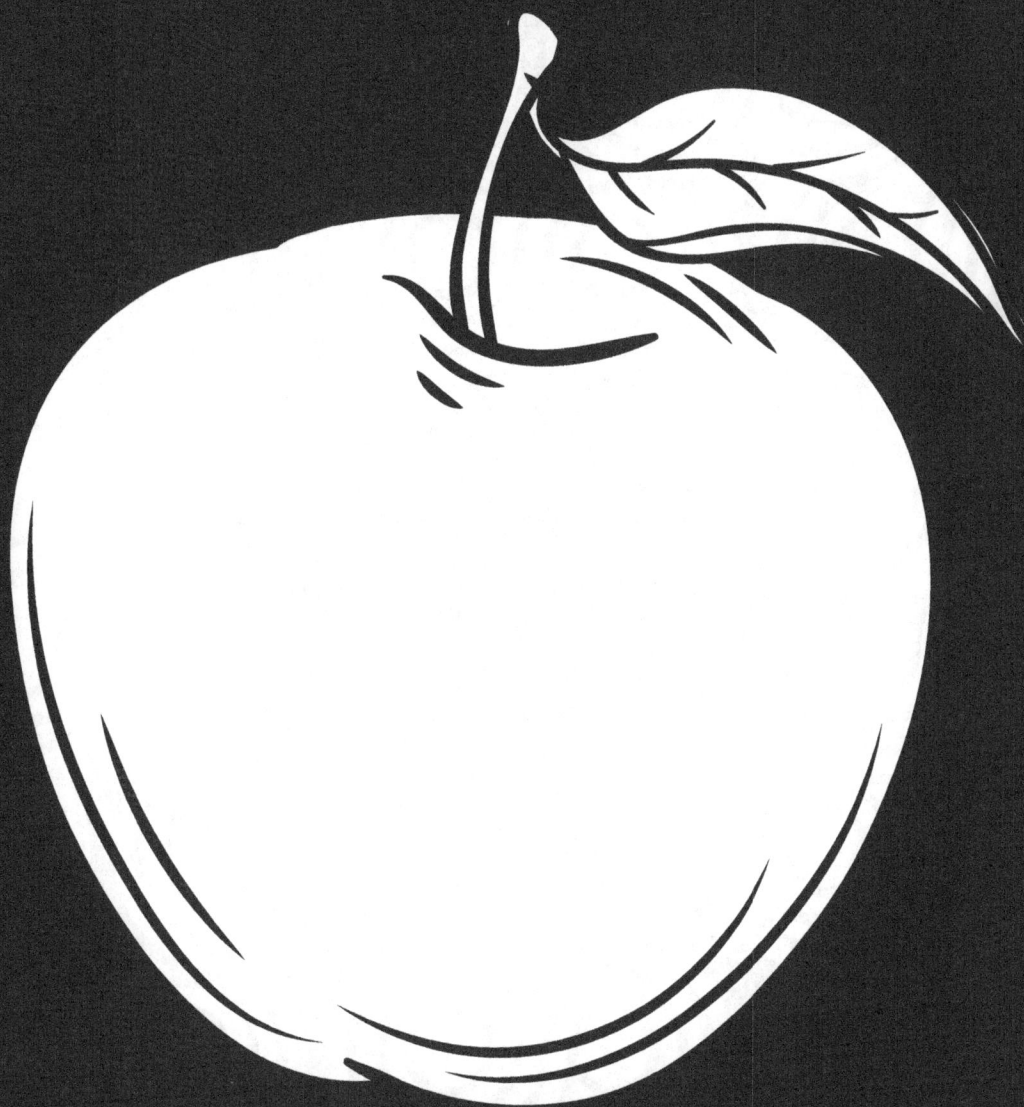

APPLE

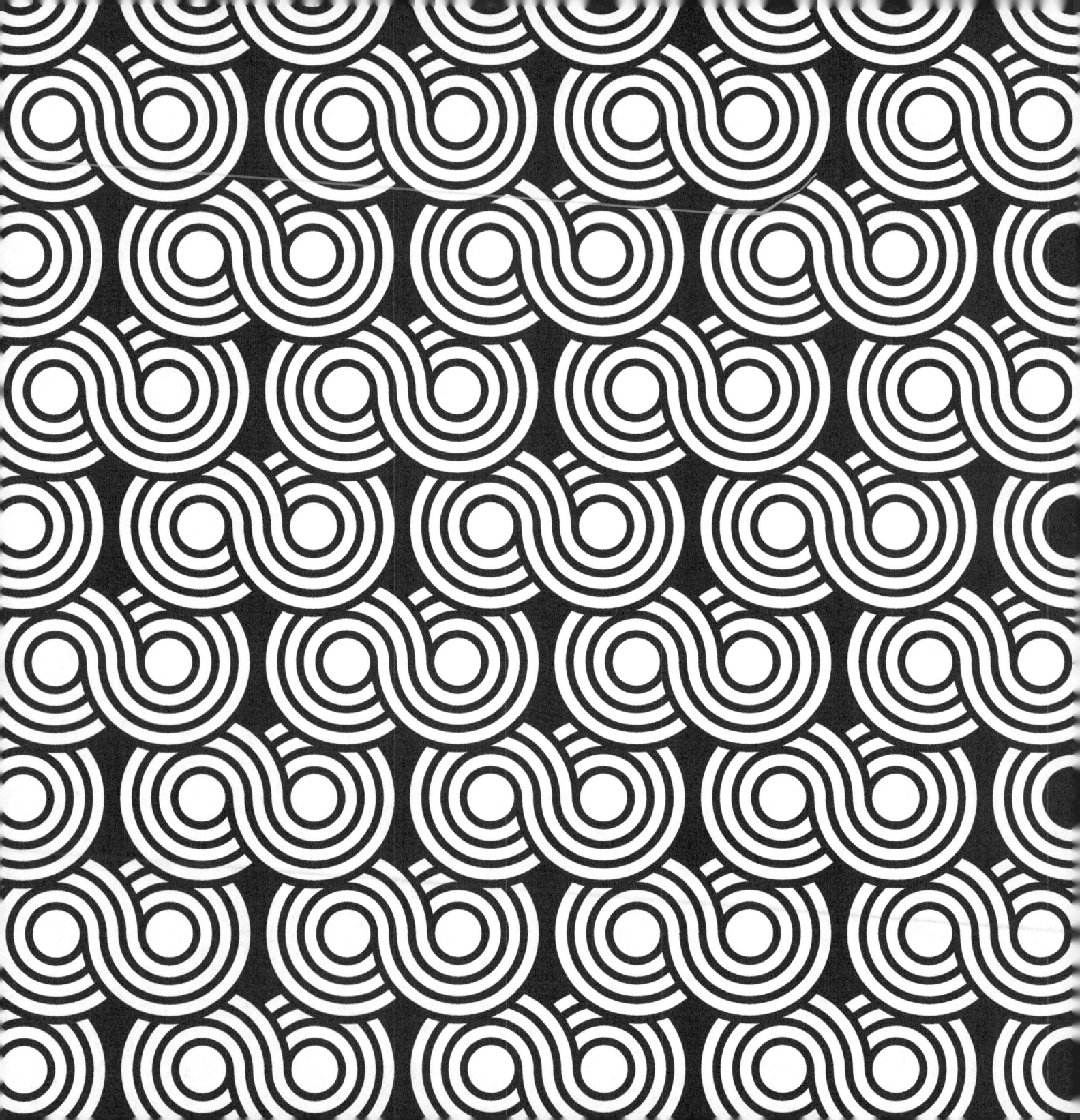

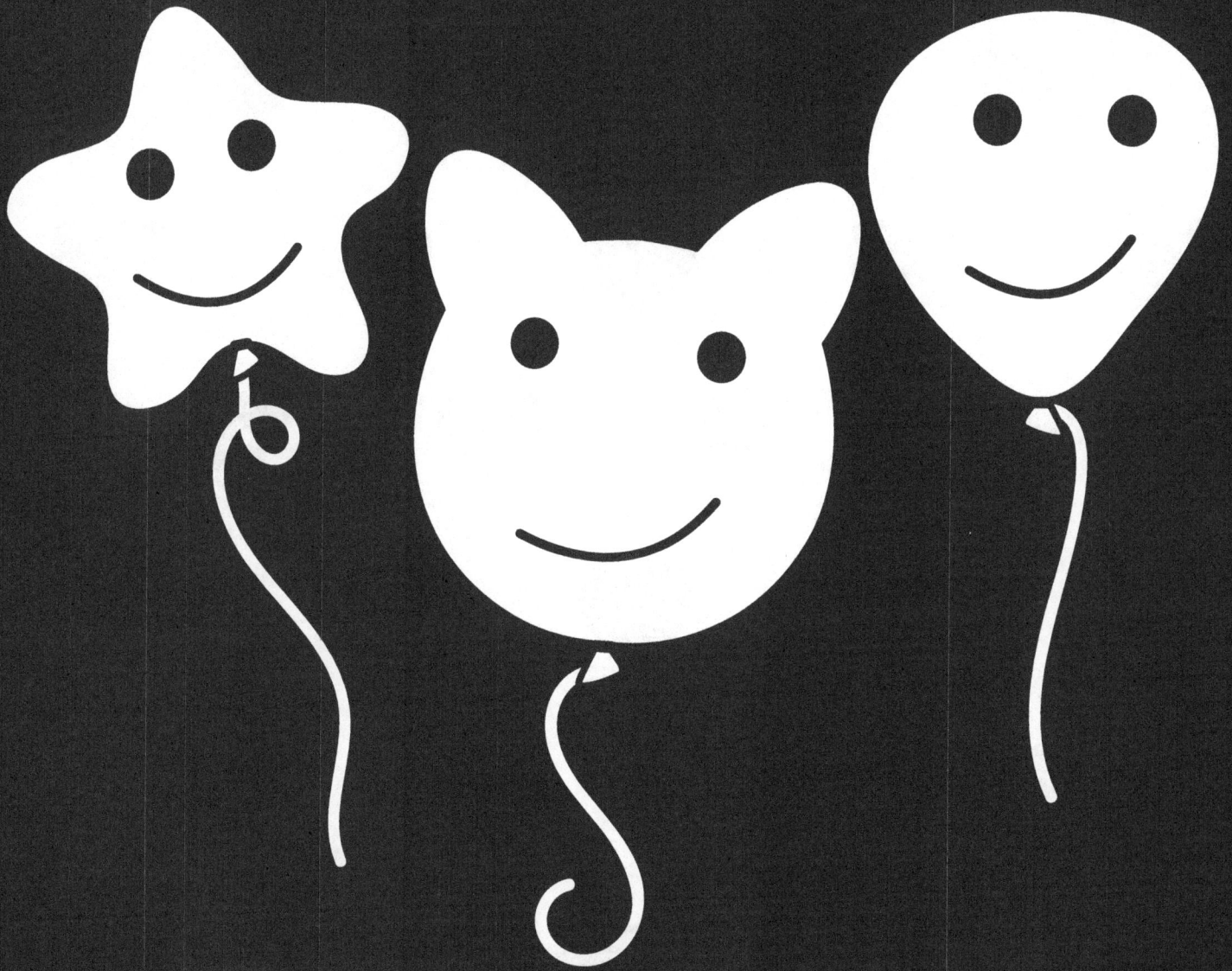

BALLOON

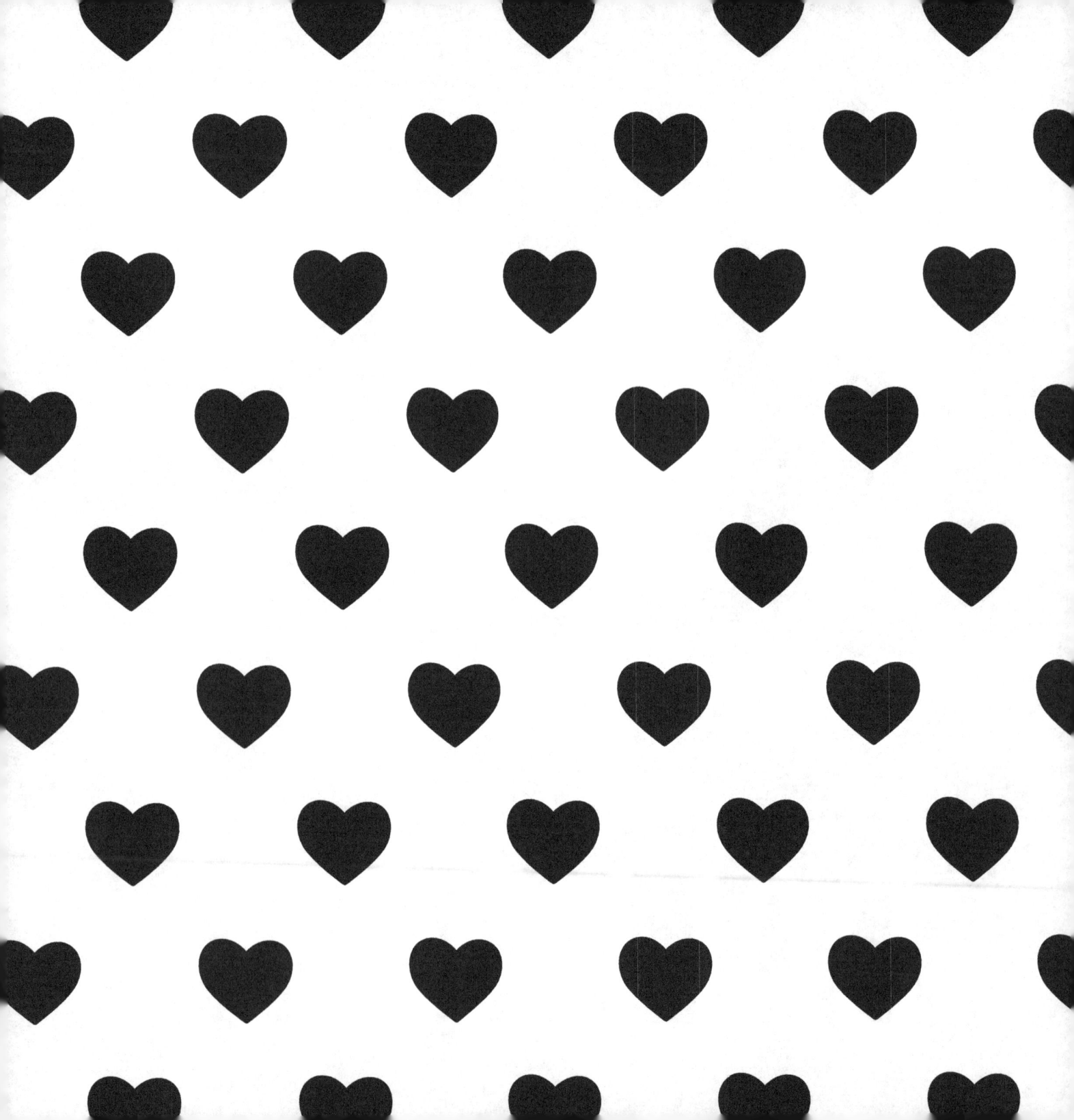

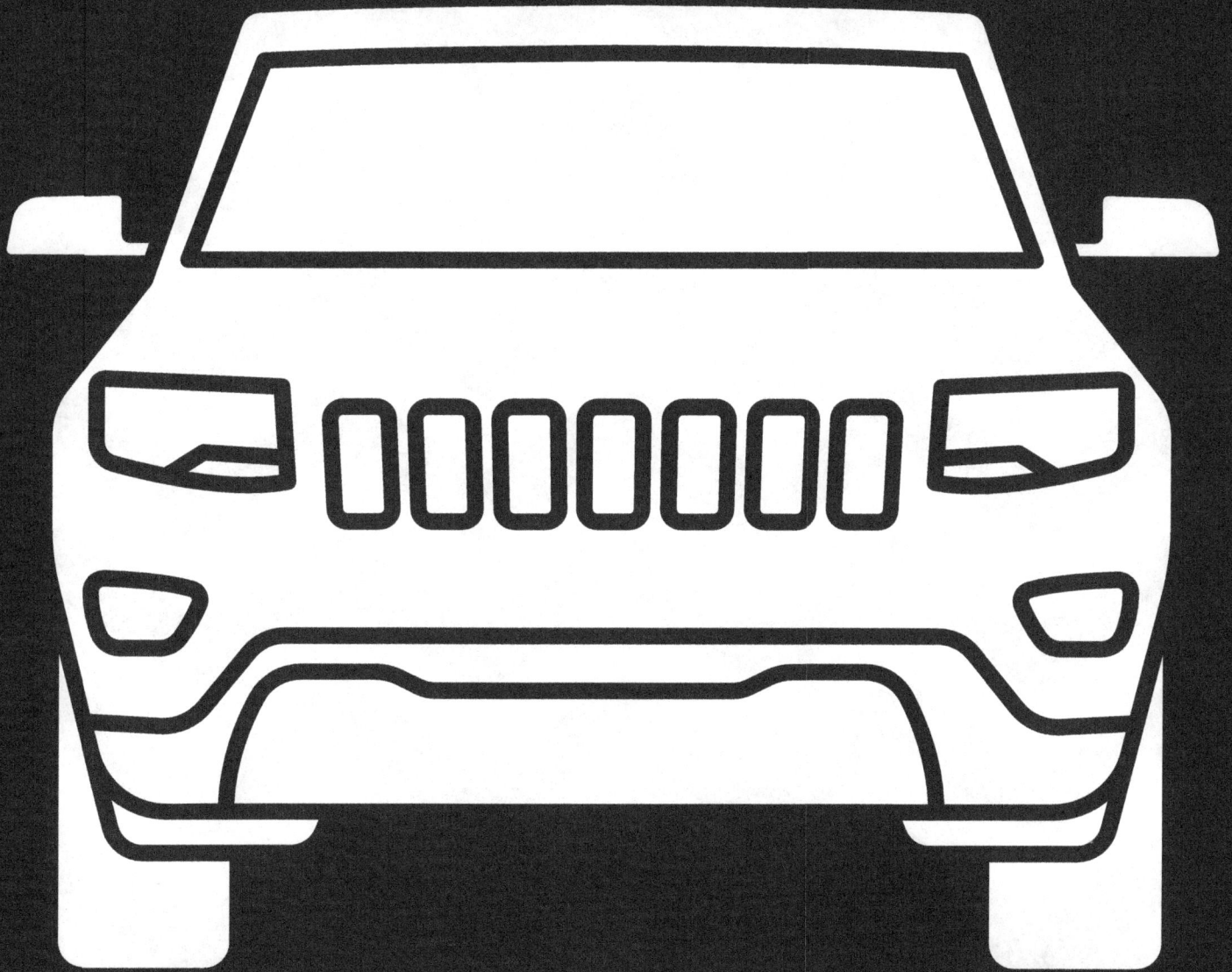

CAR

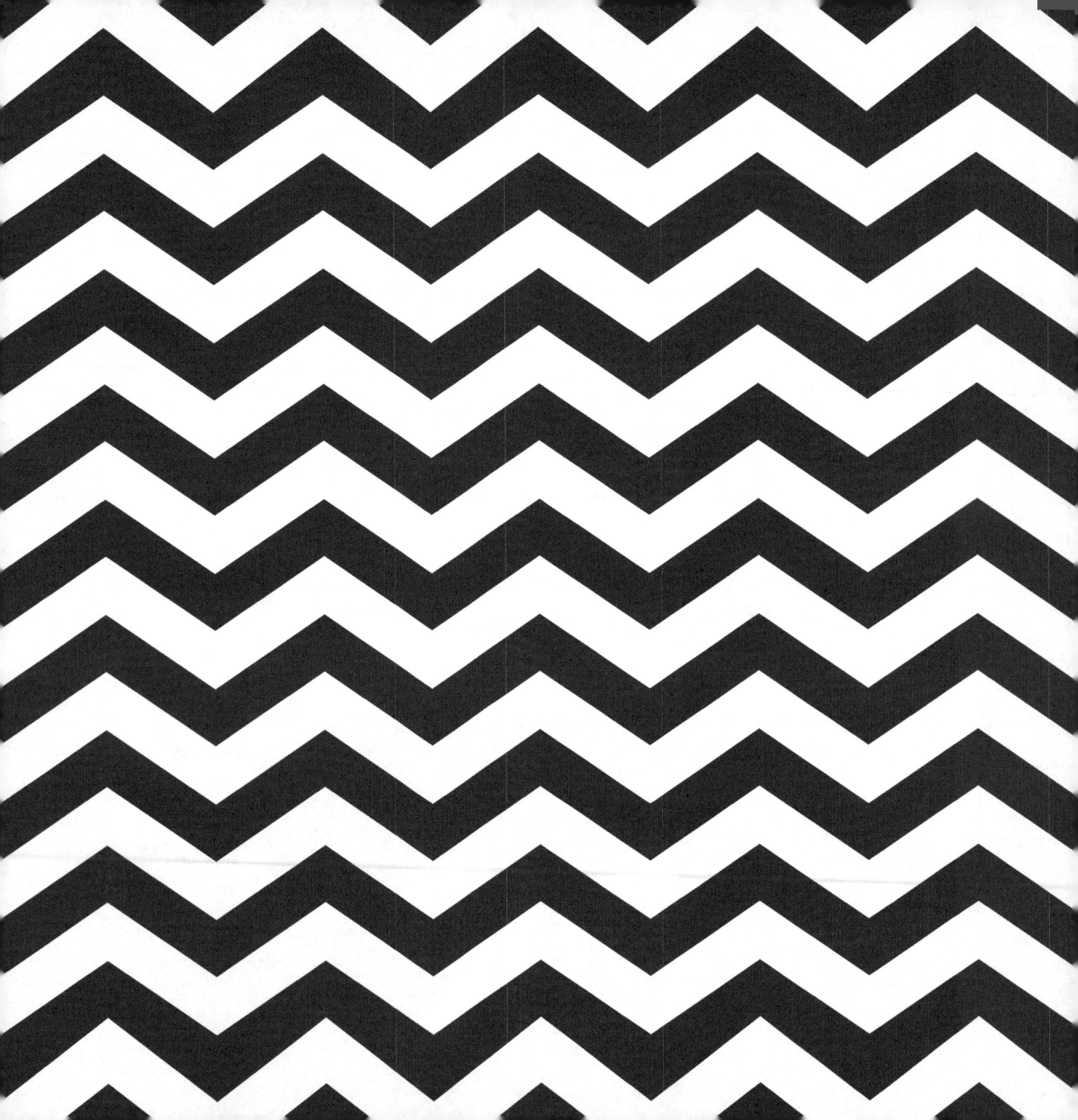

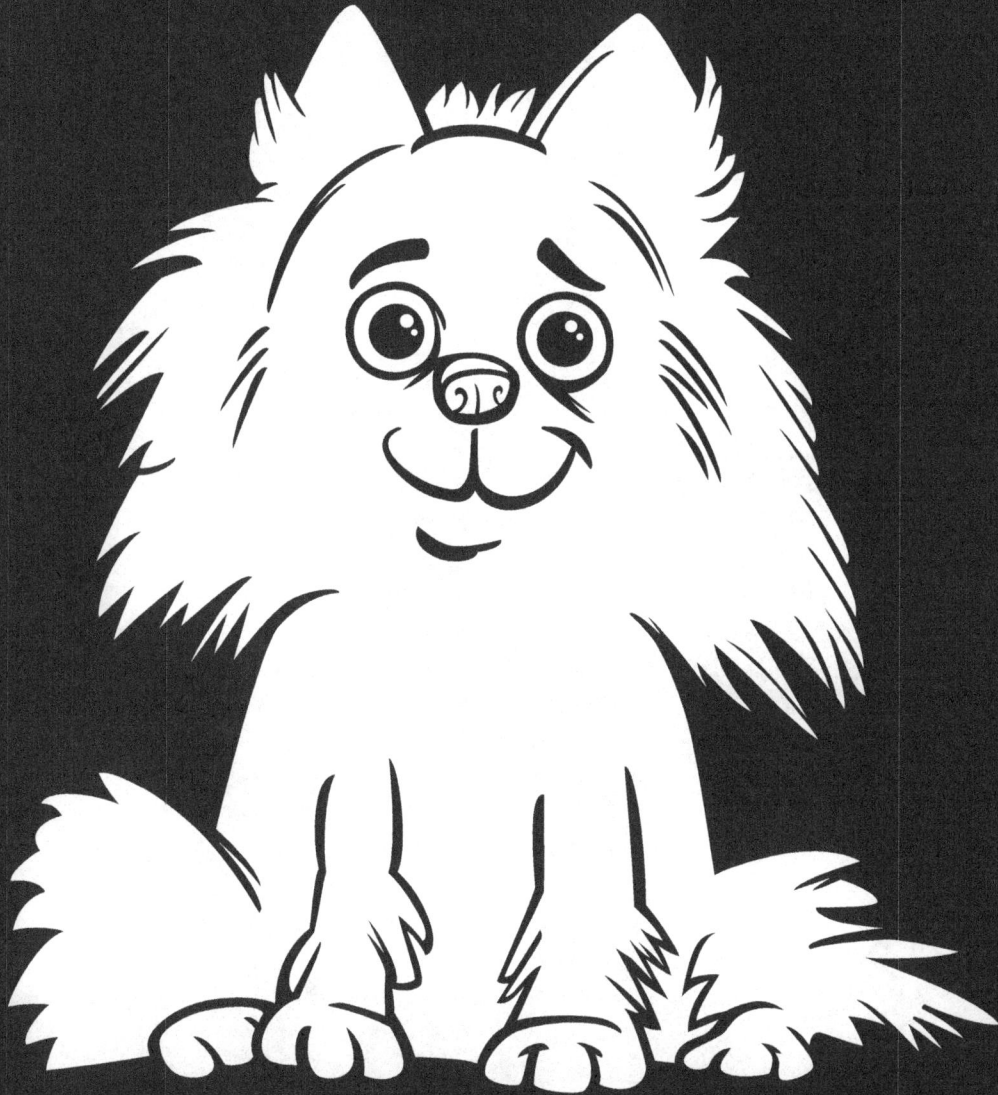

DOG

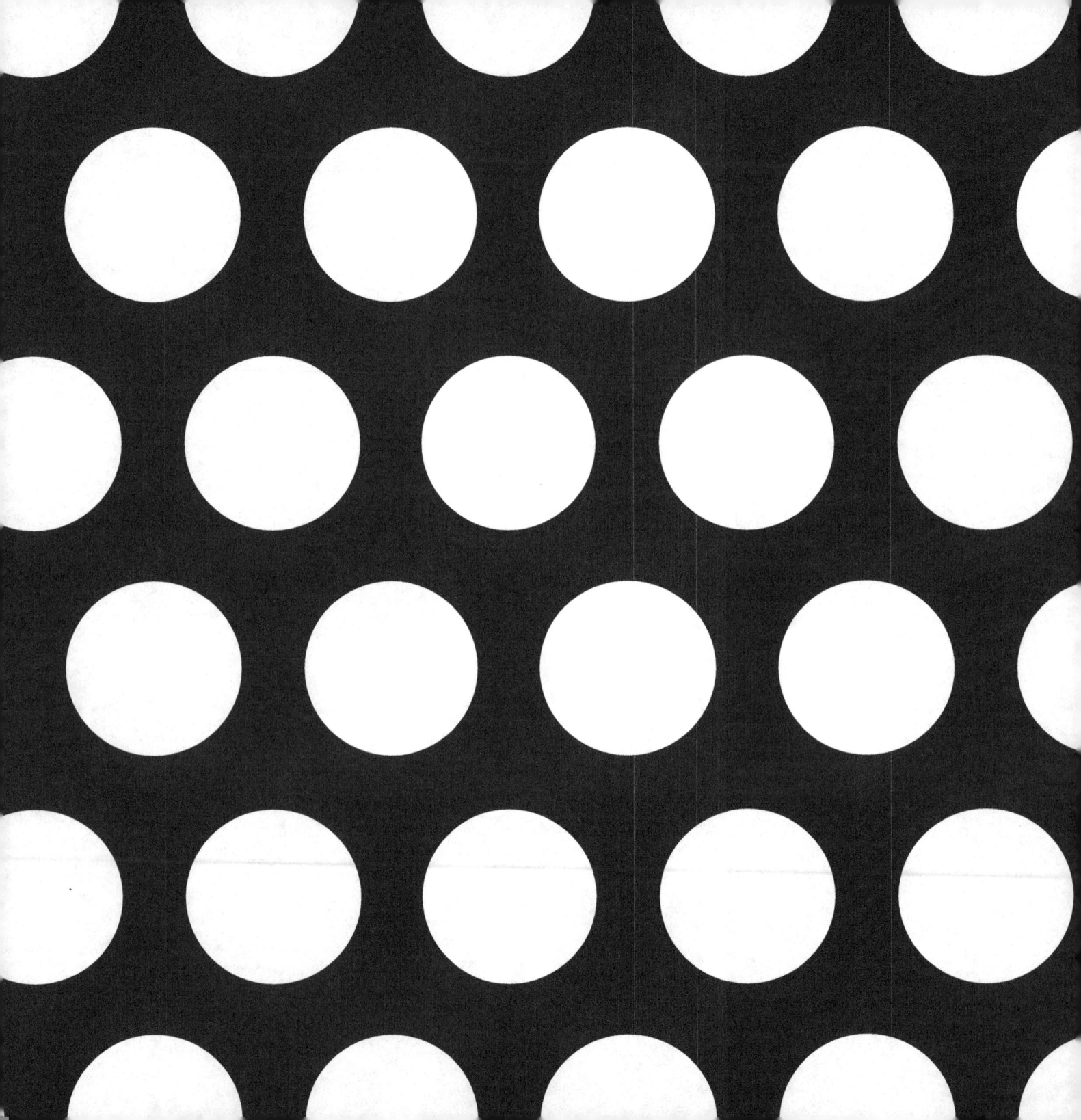

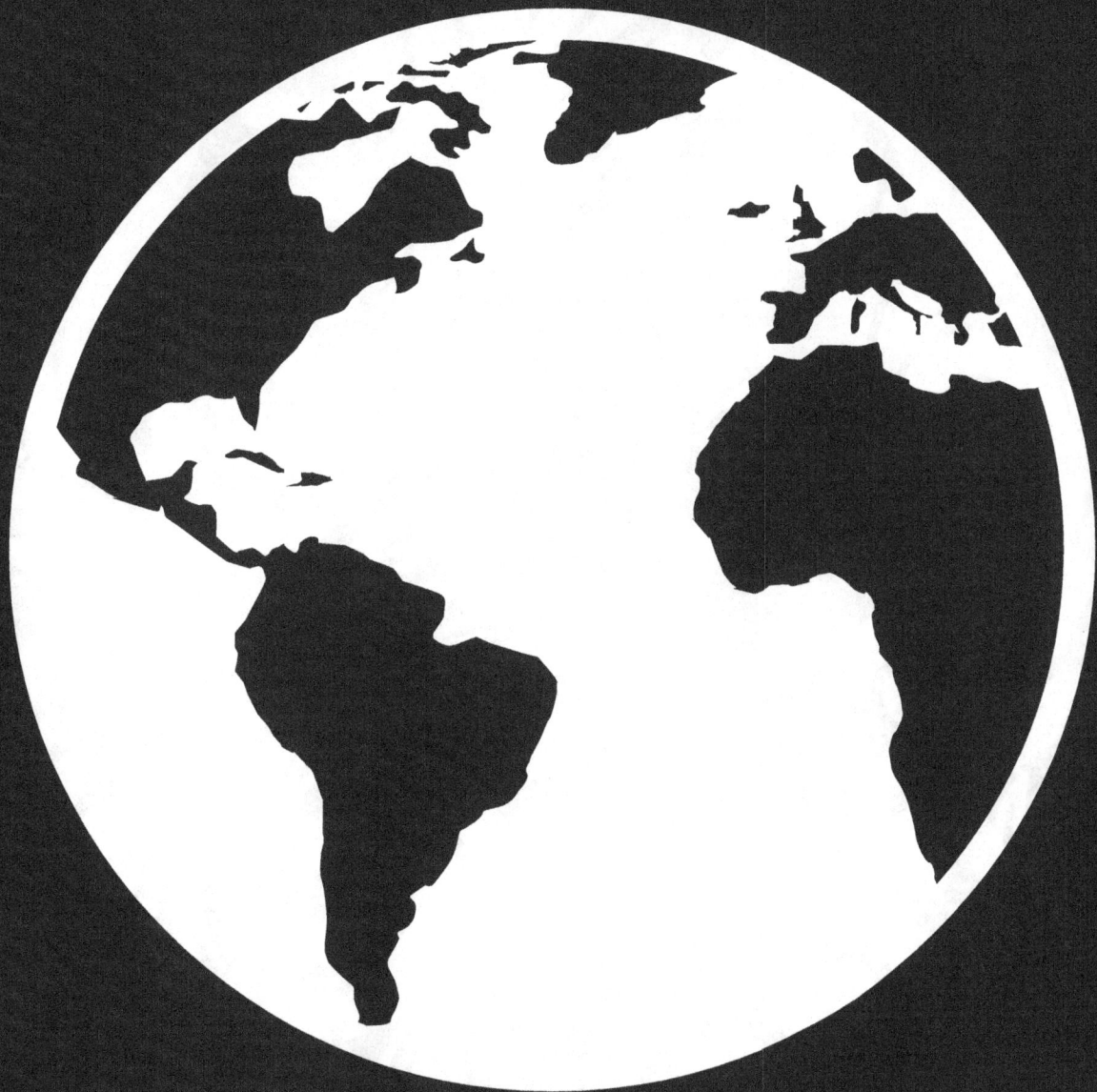

Earth

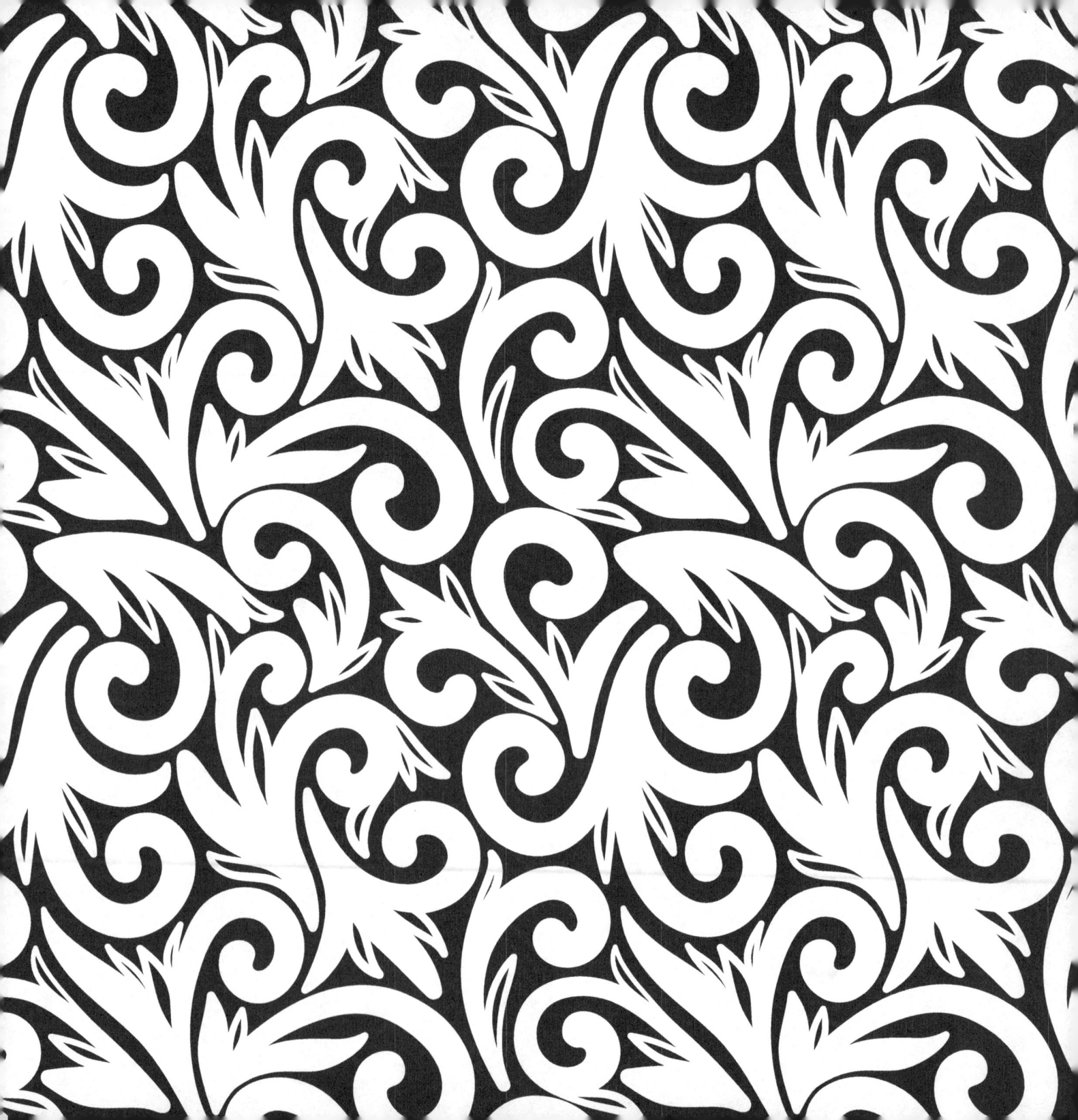

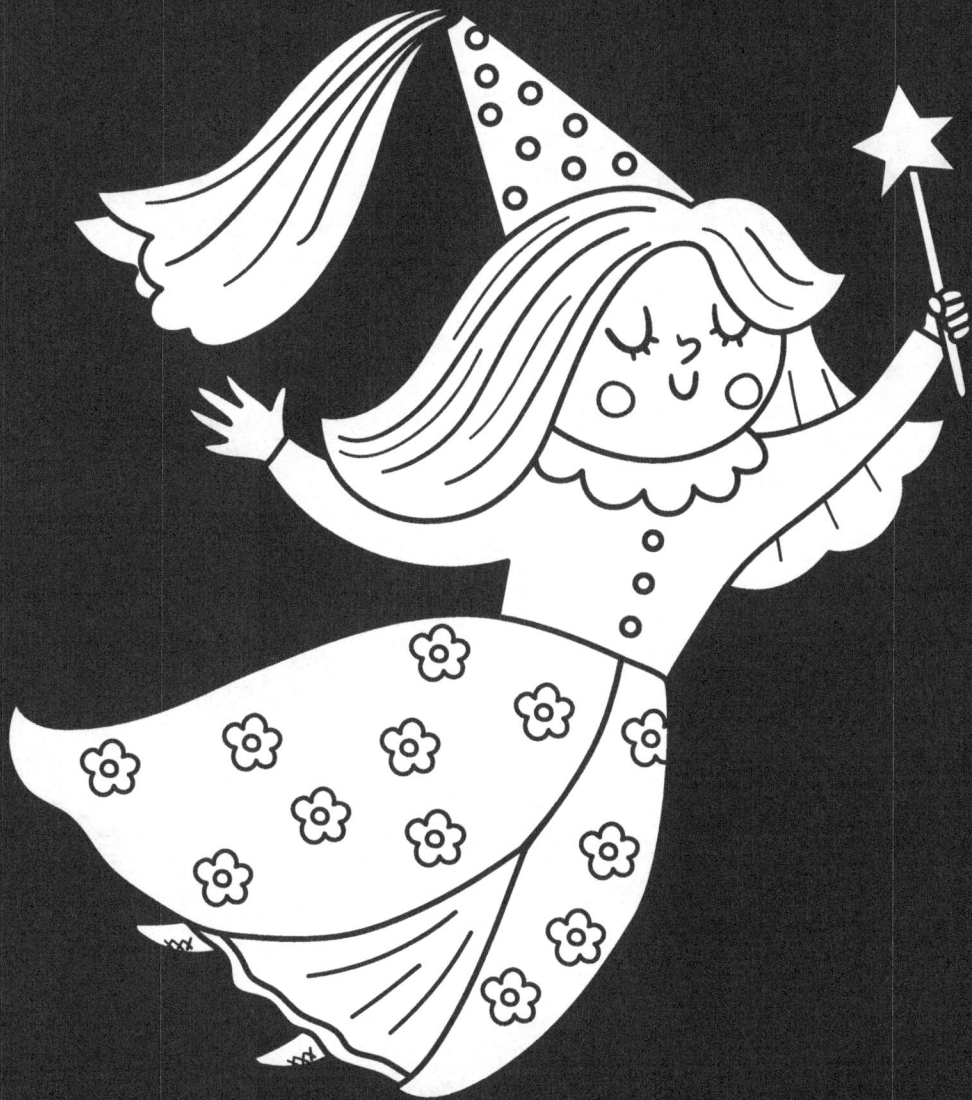

Fairy

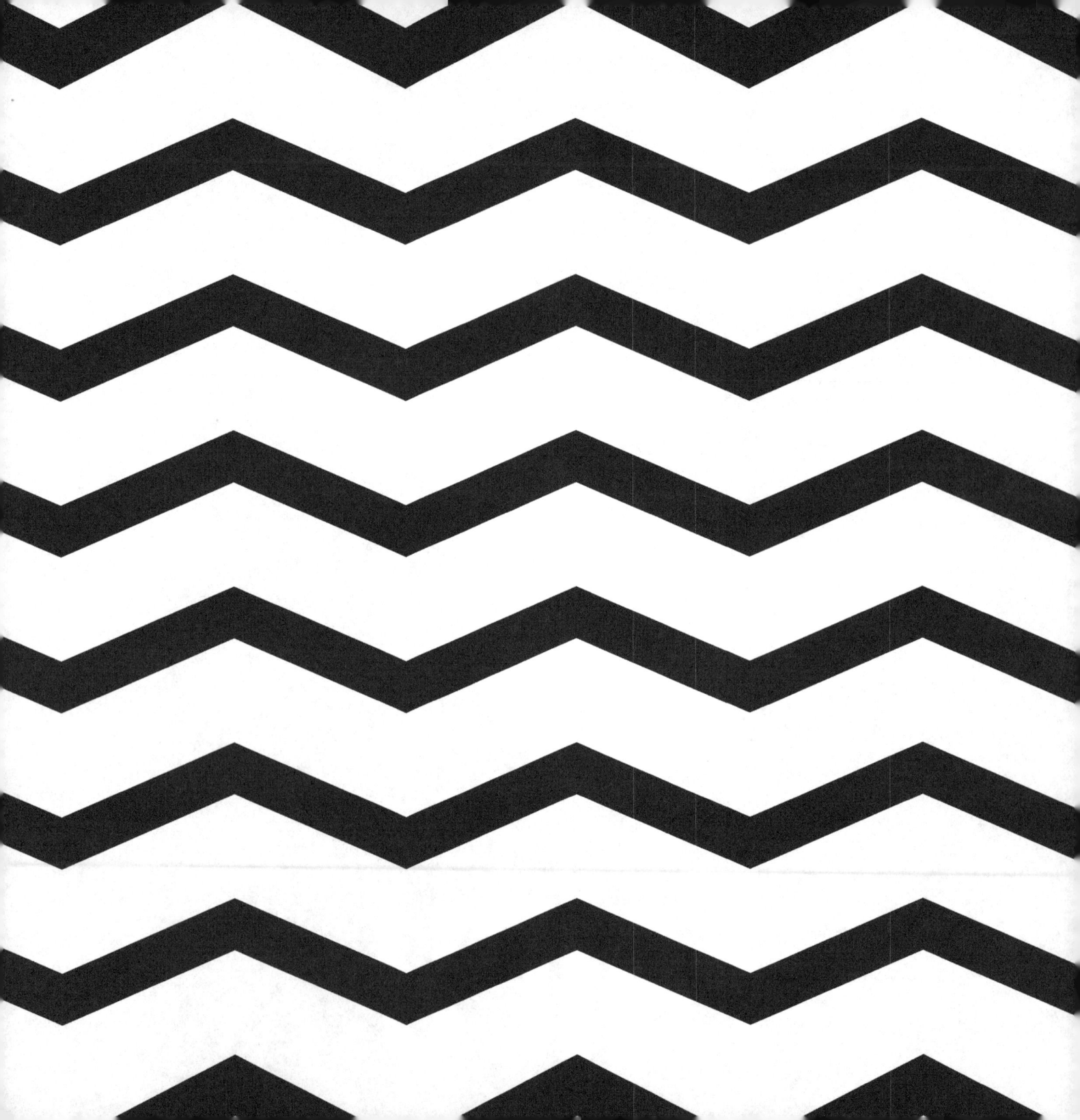

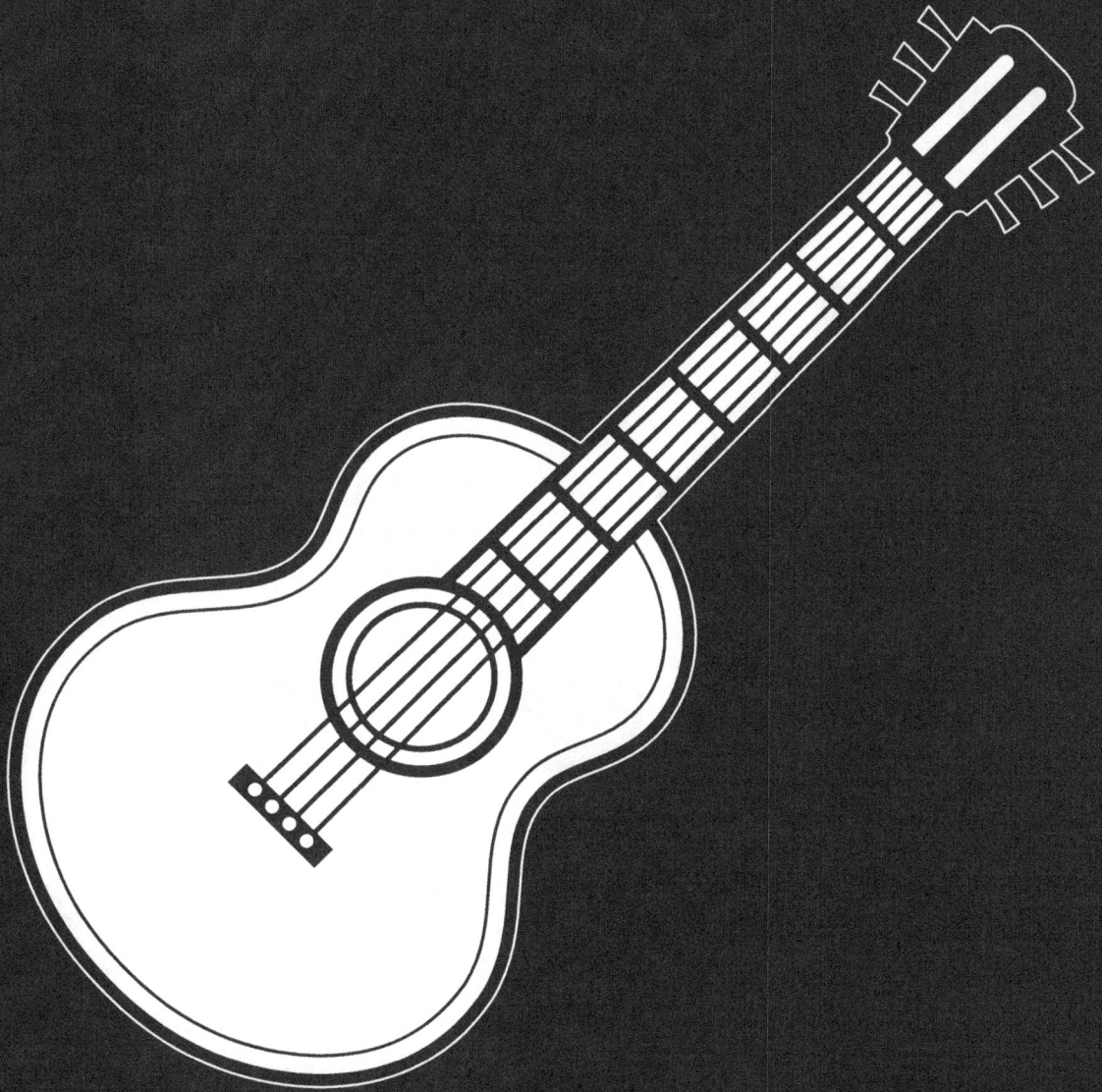

GUITAR

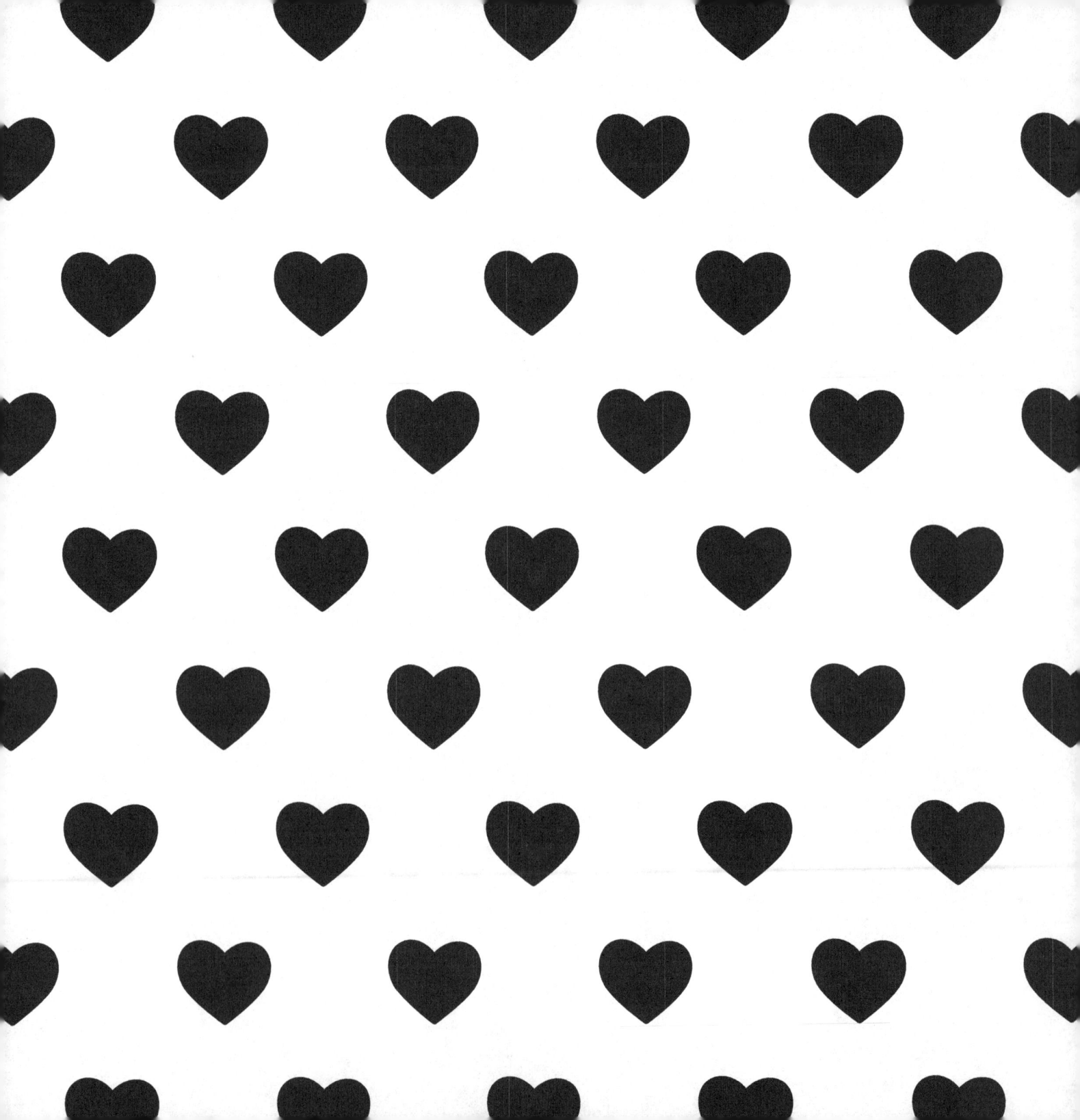

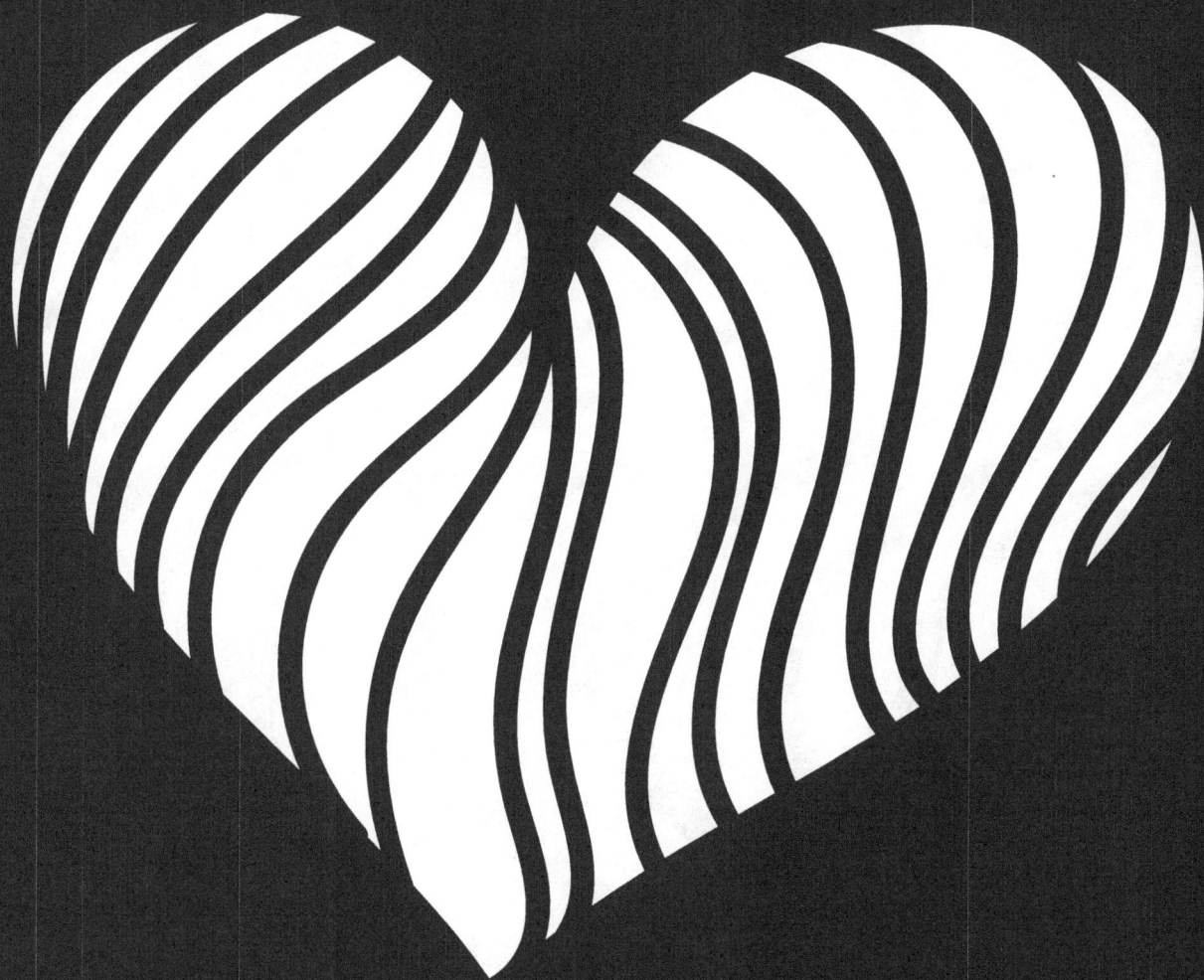

HEART

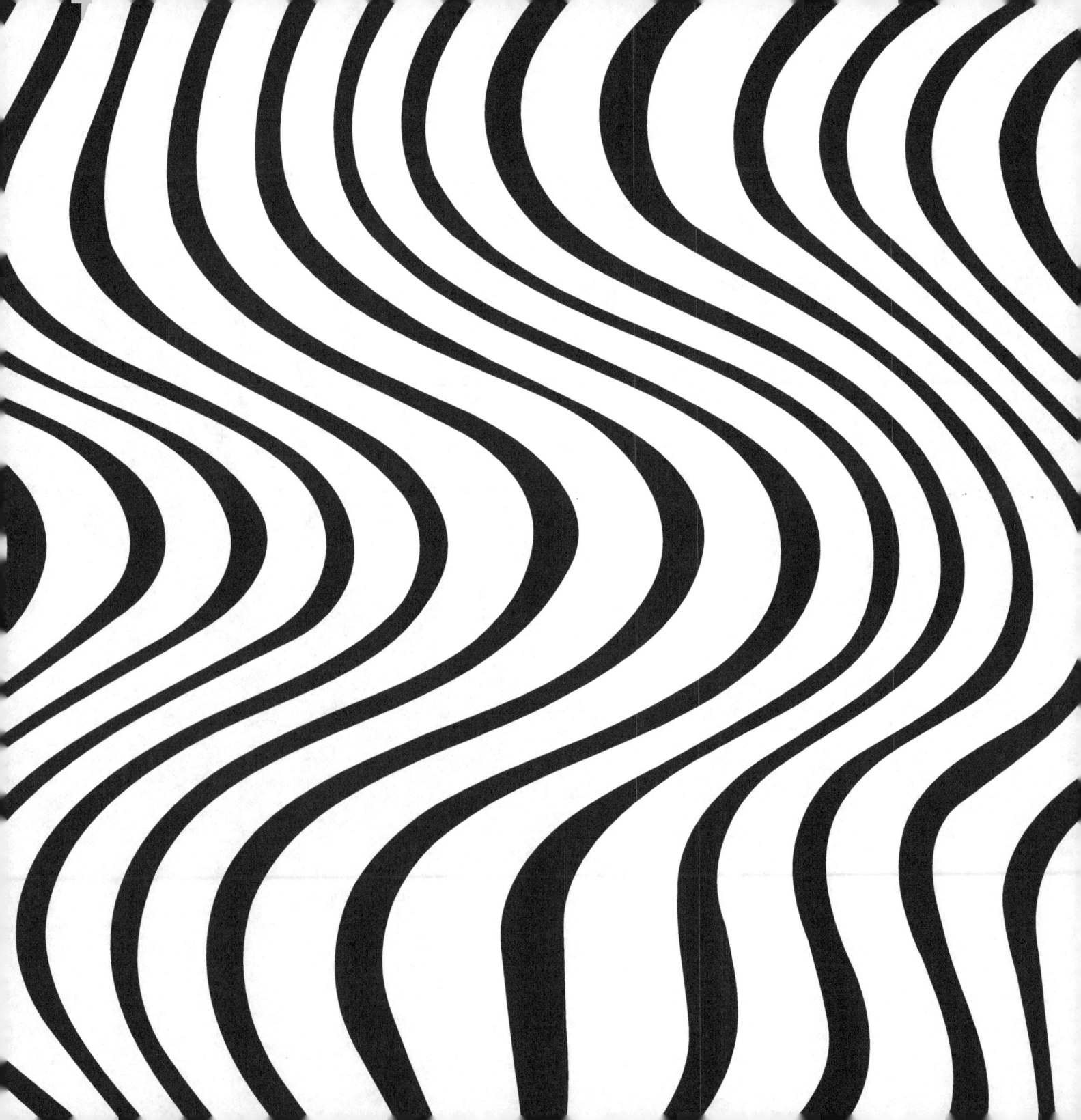

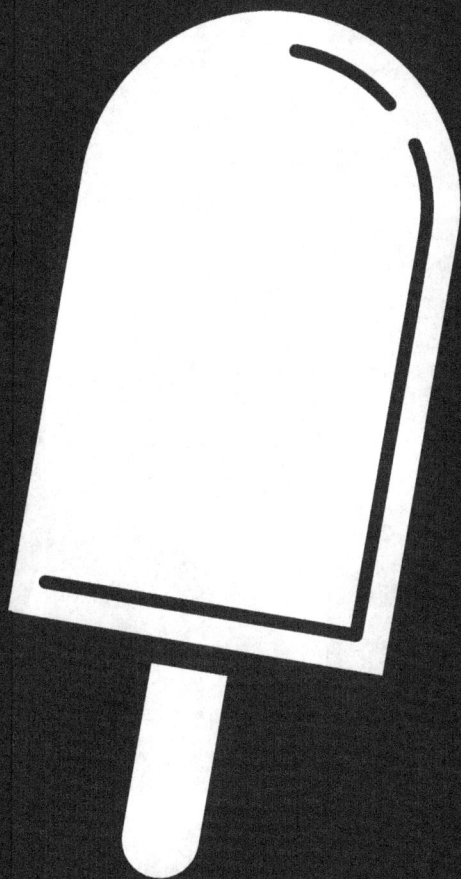

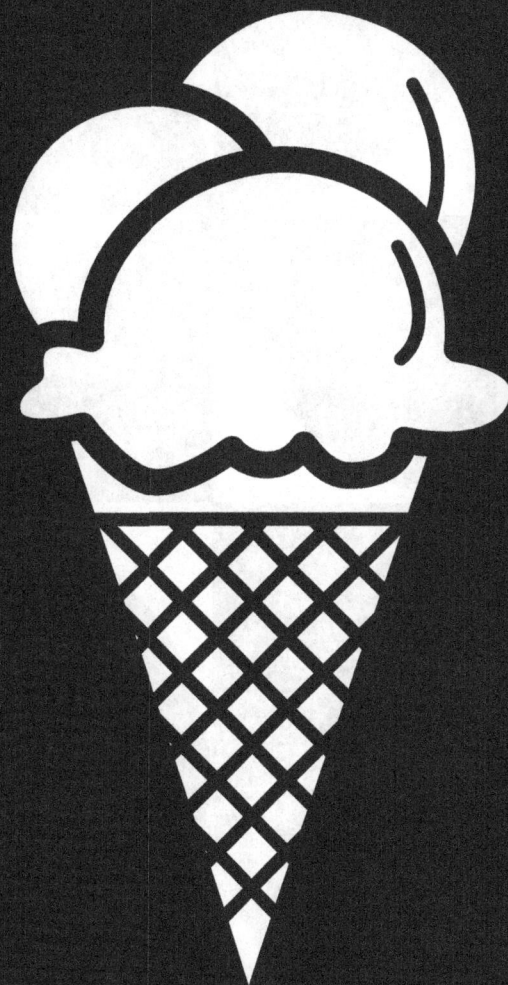

ICE CREAM

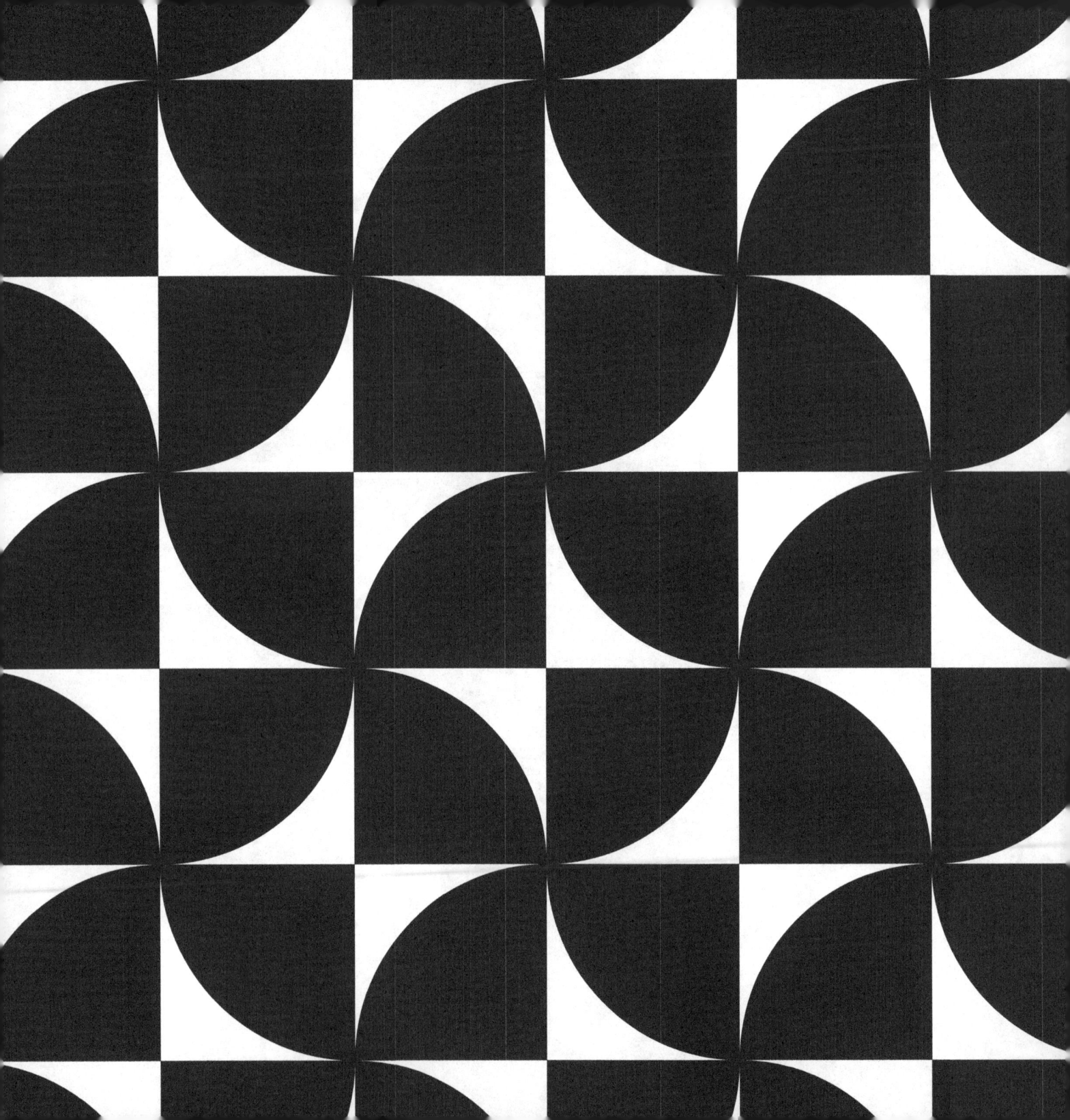

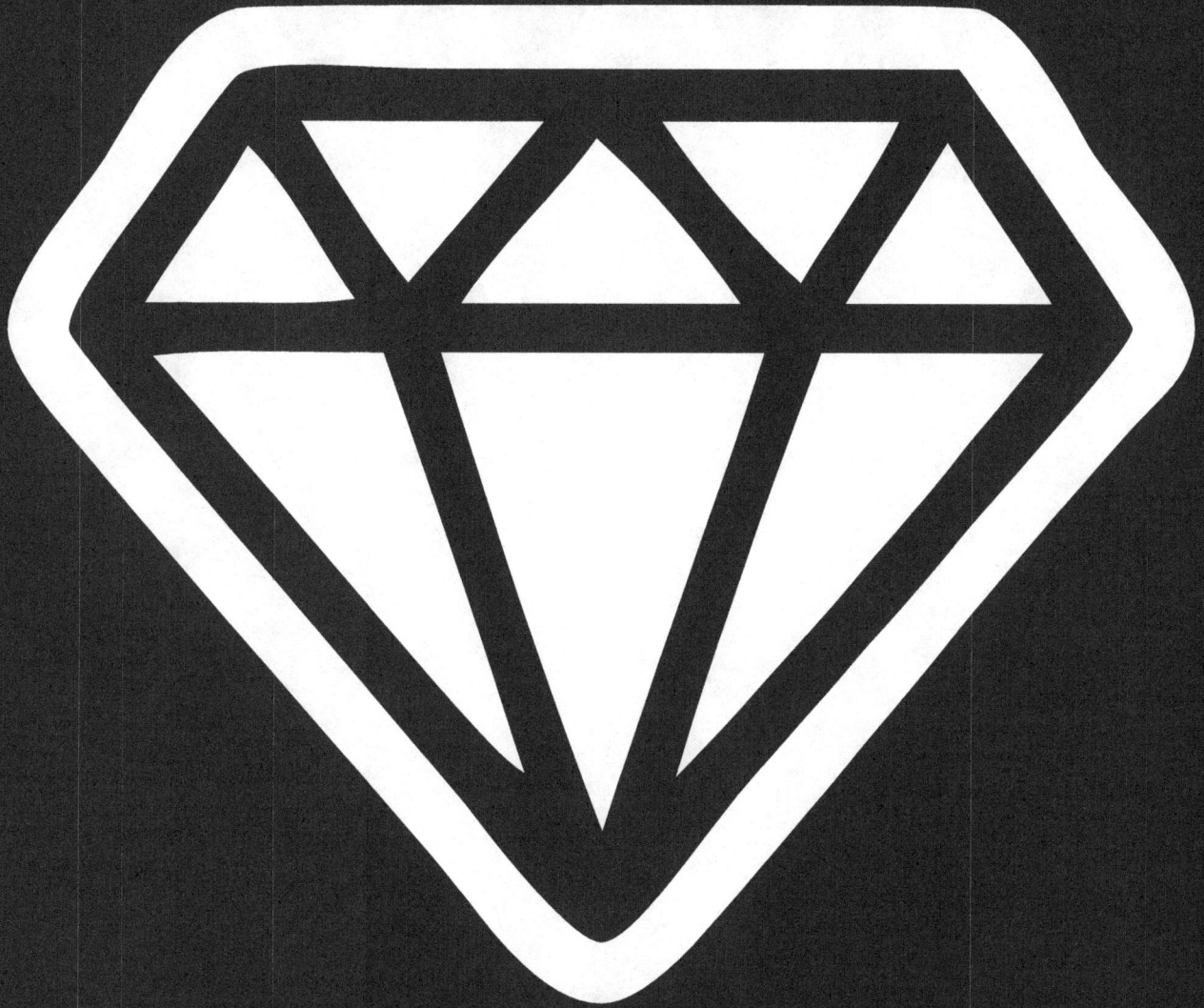

JEWELRY

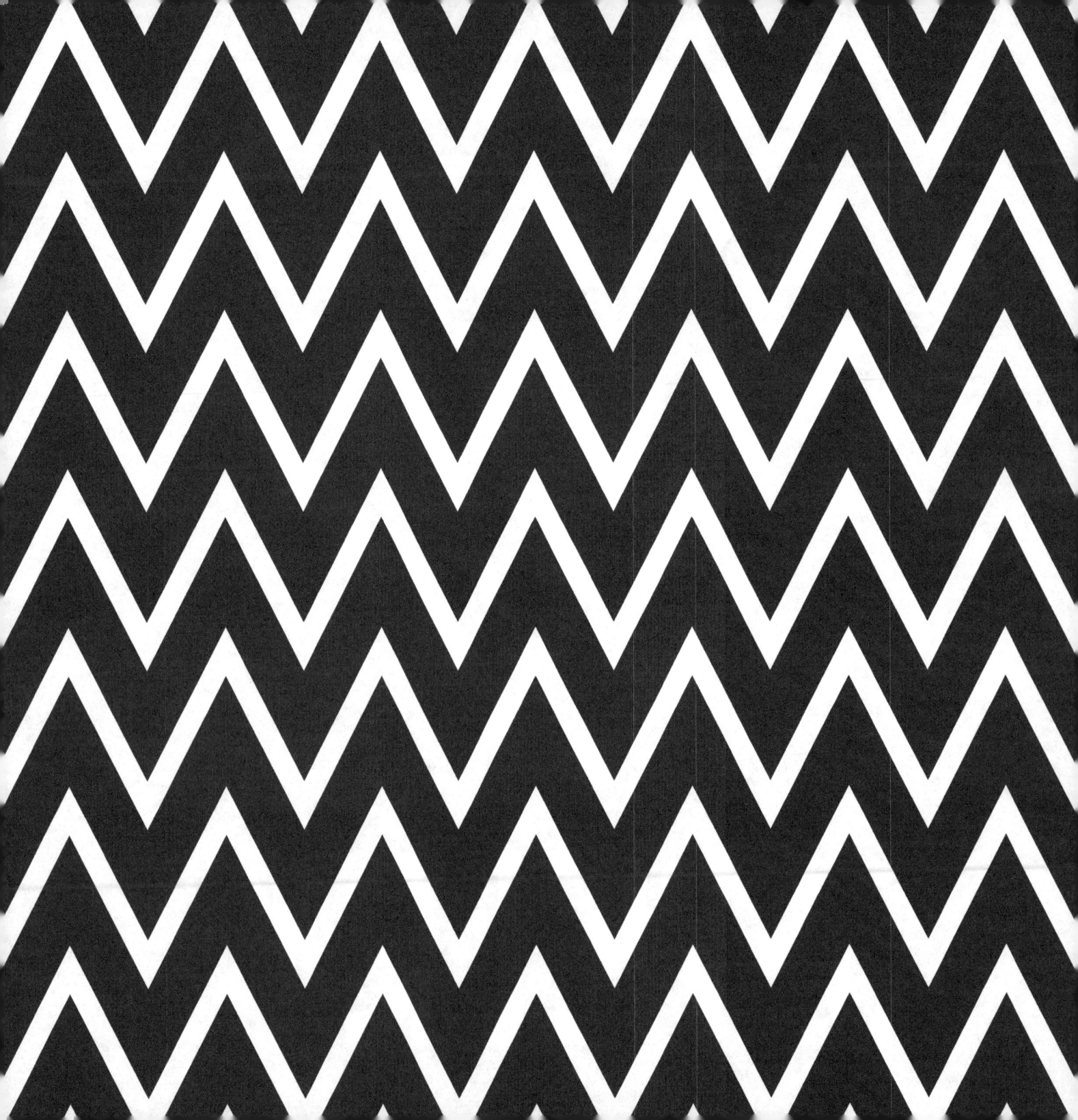

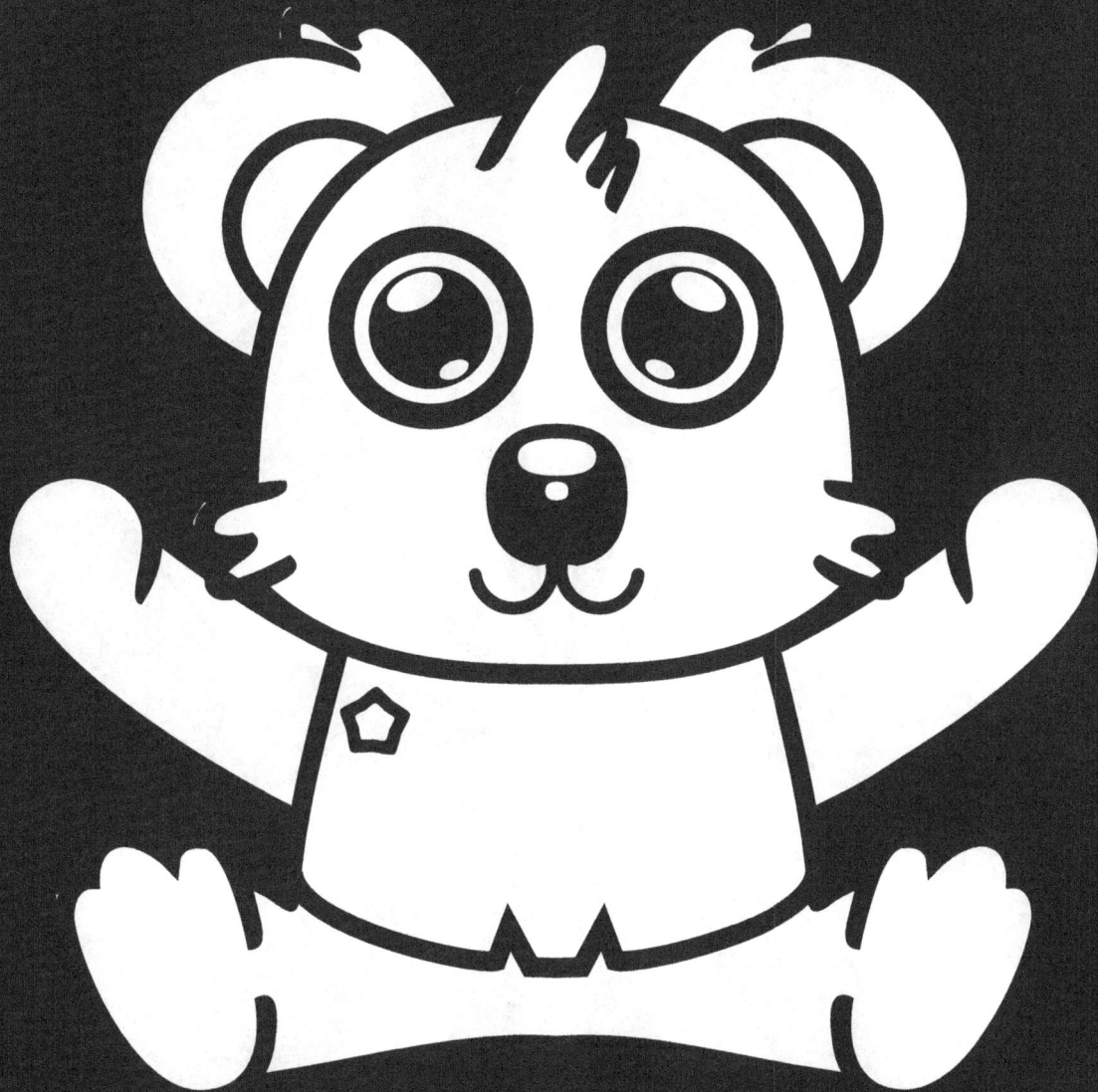

KOALA

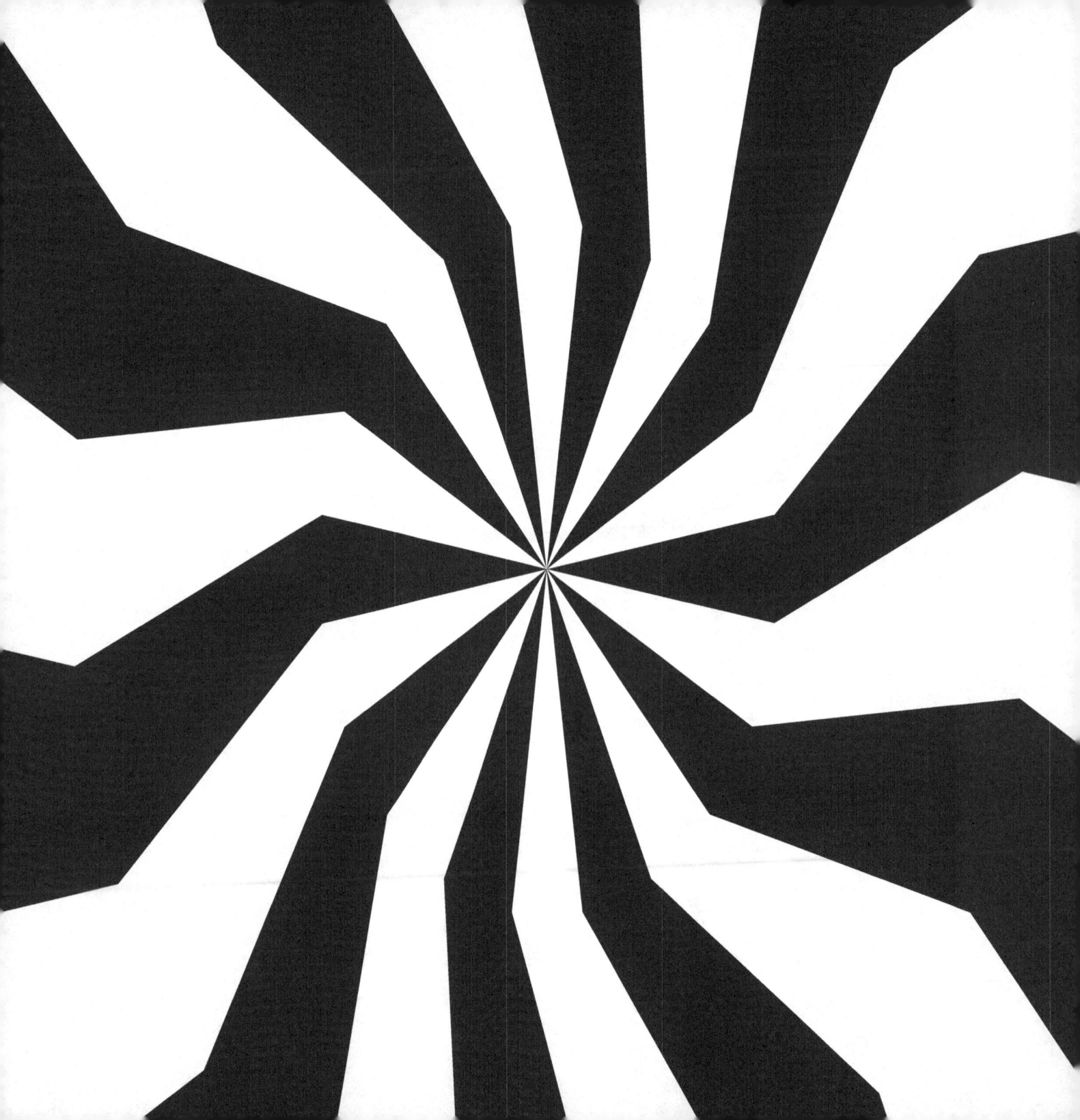

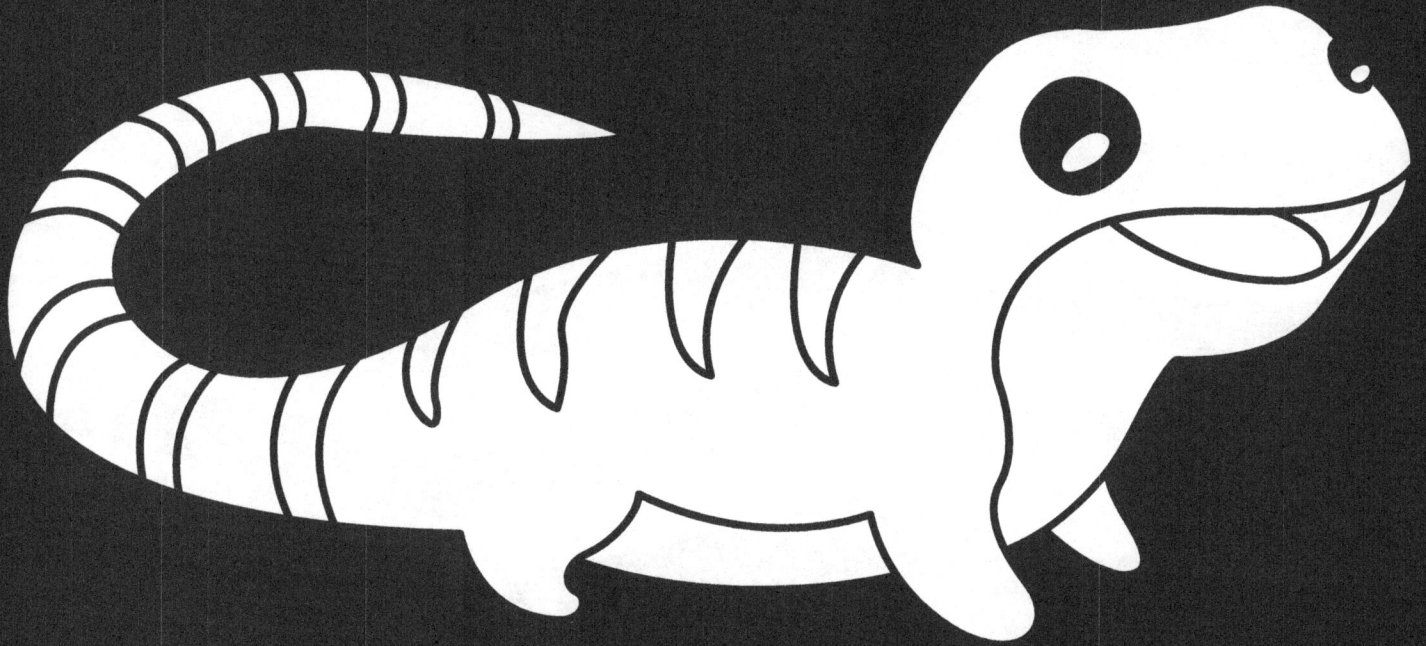

LIZARD

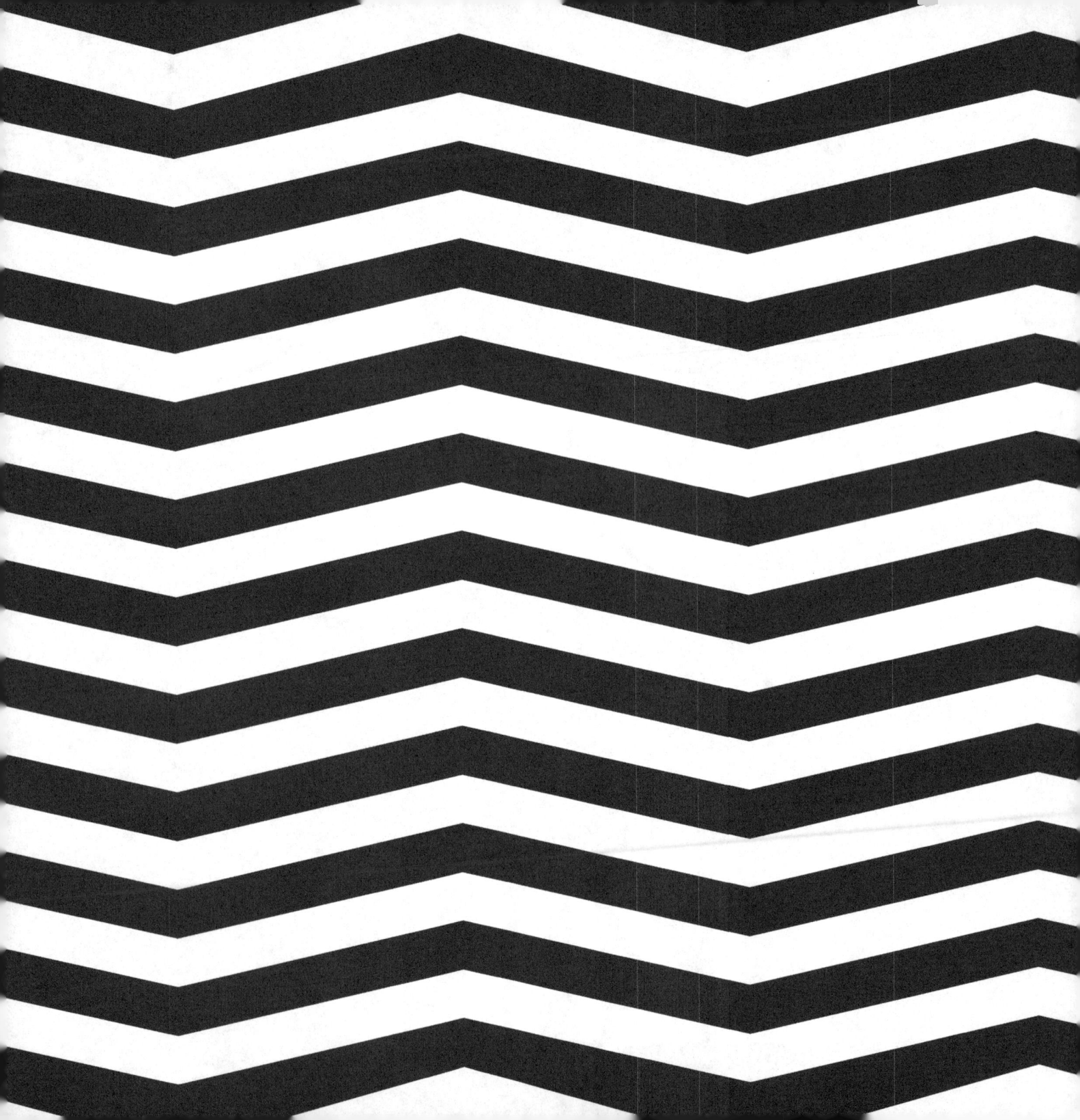

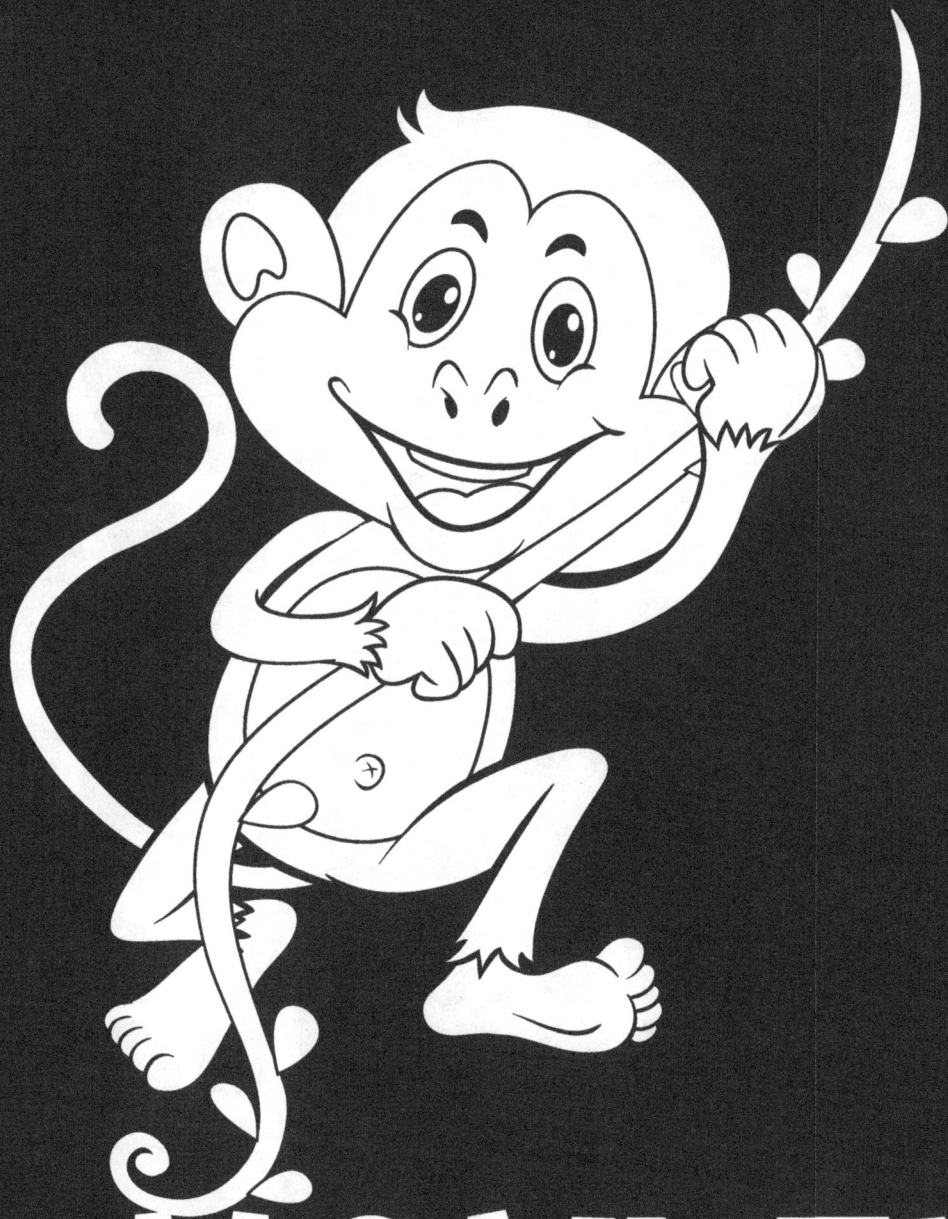

MONKEY

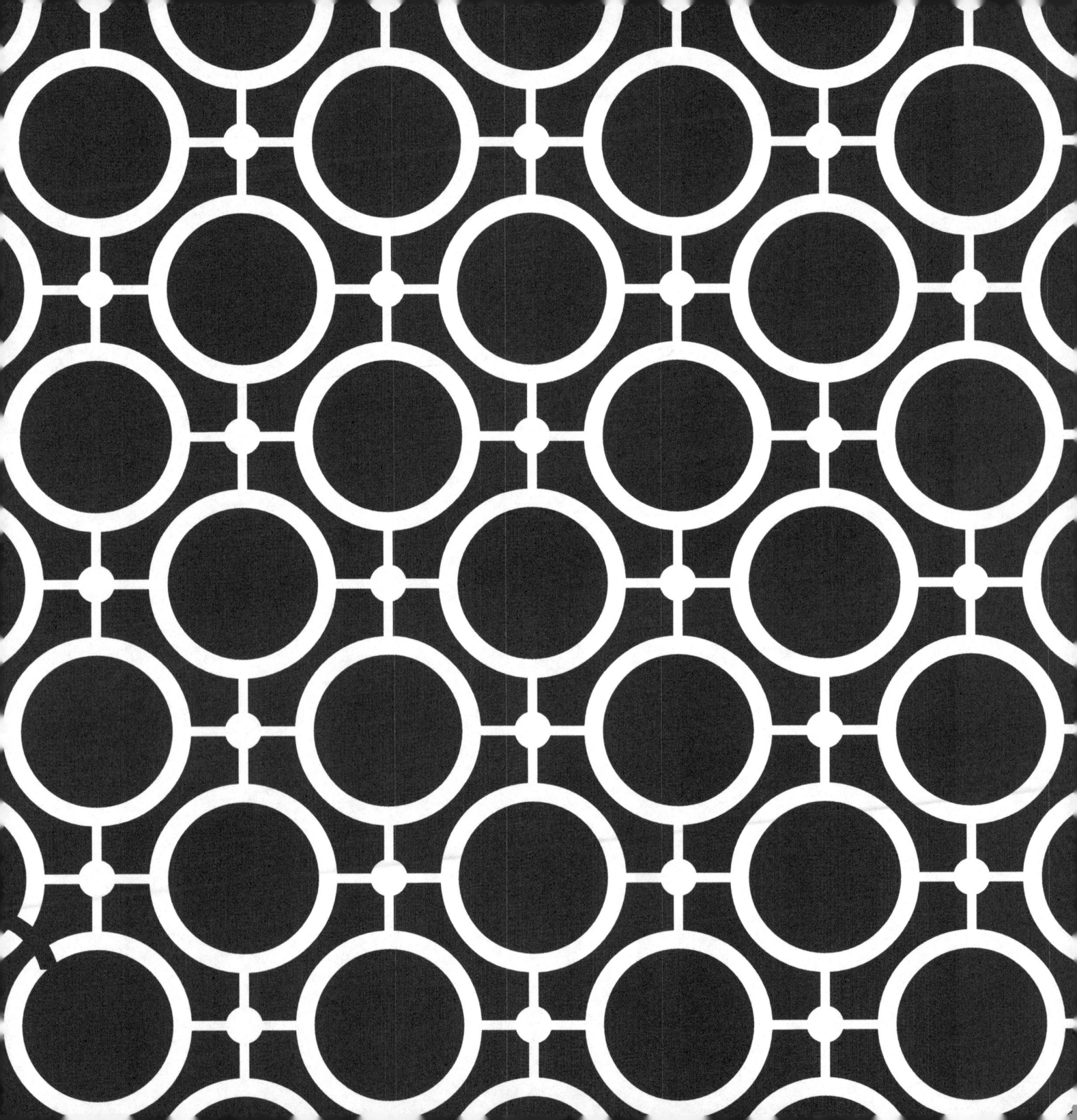

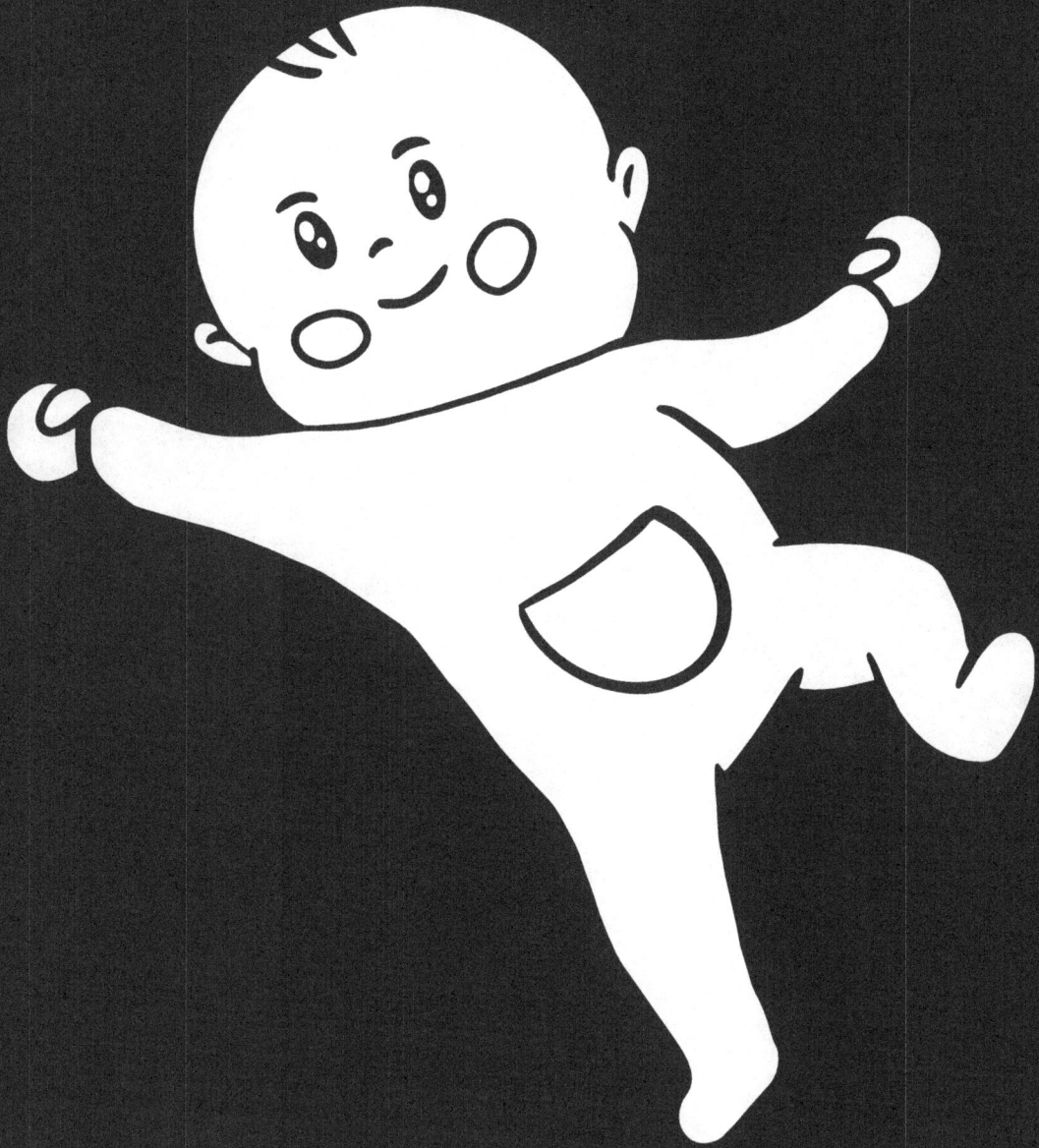

NEWBORN

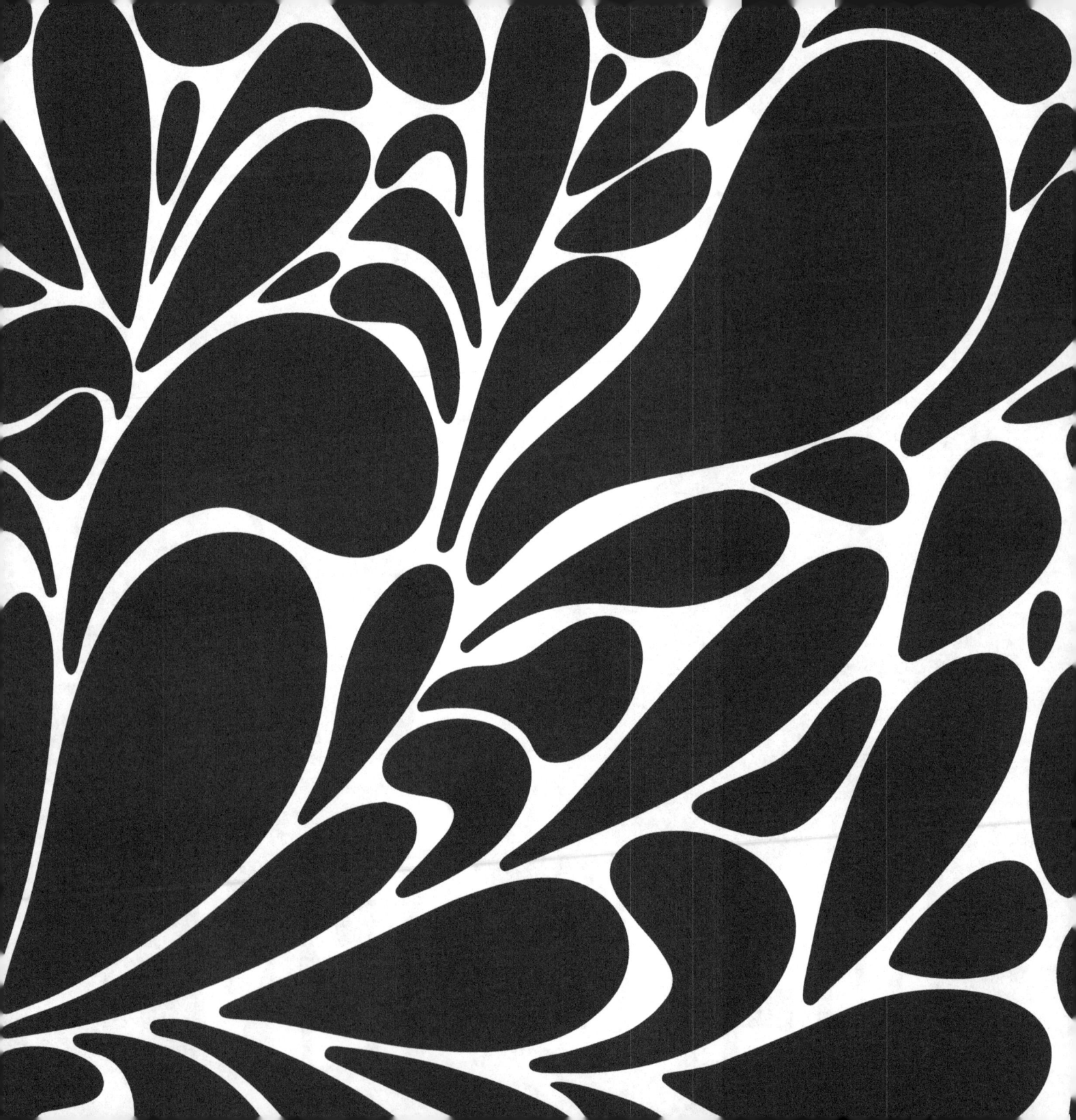

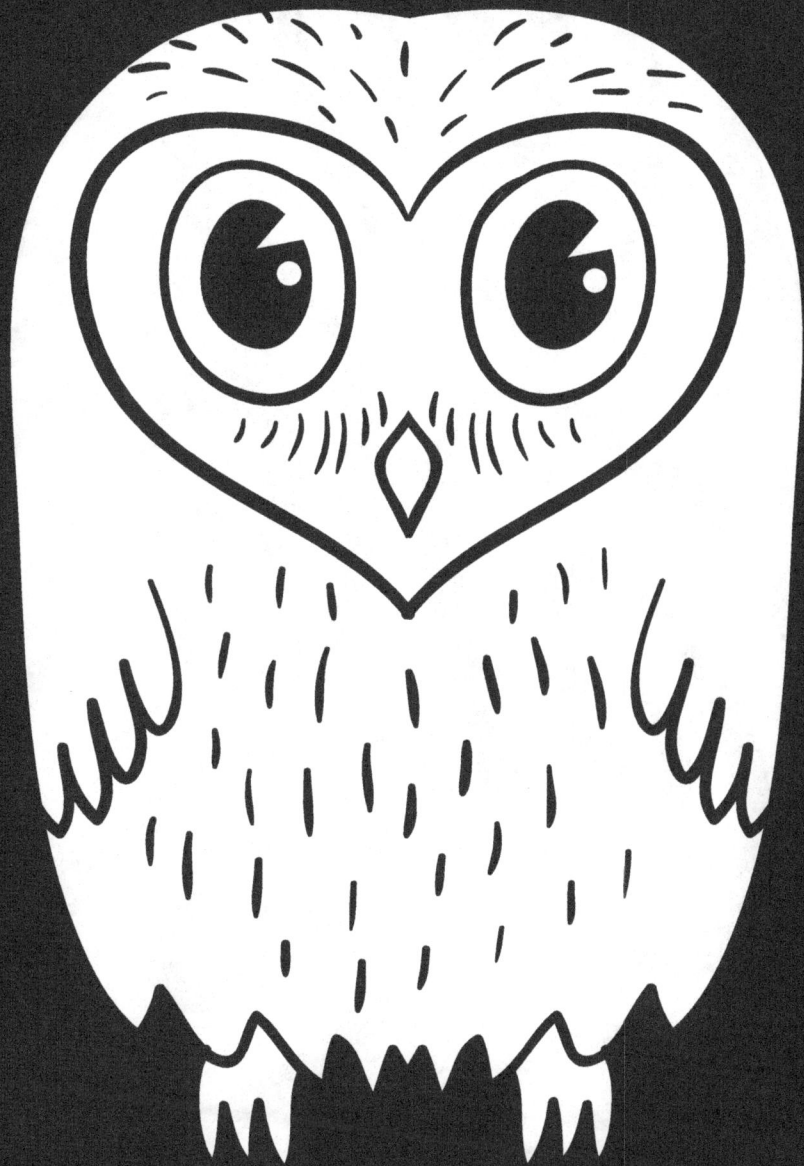

OWL

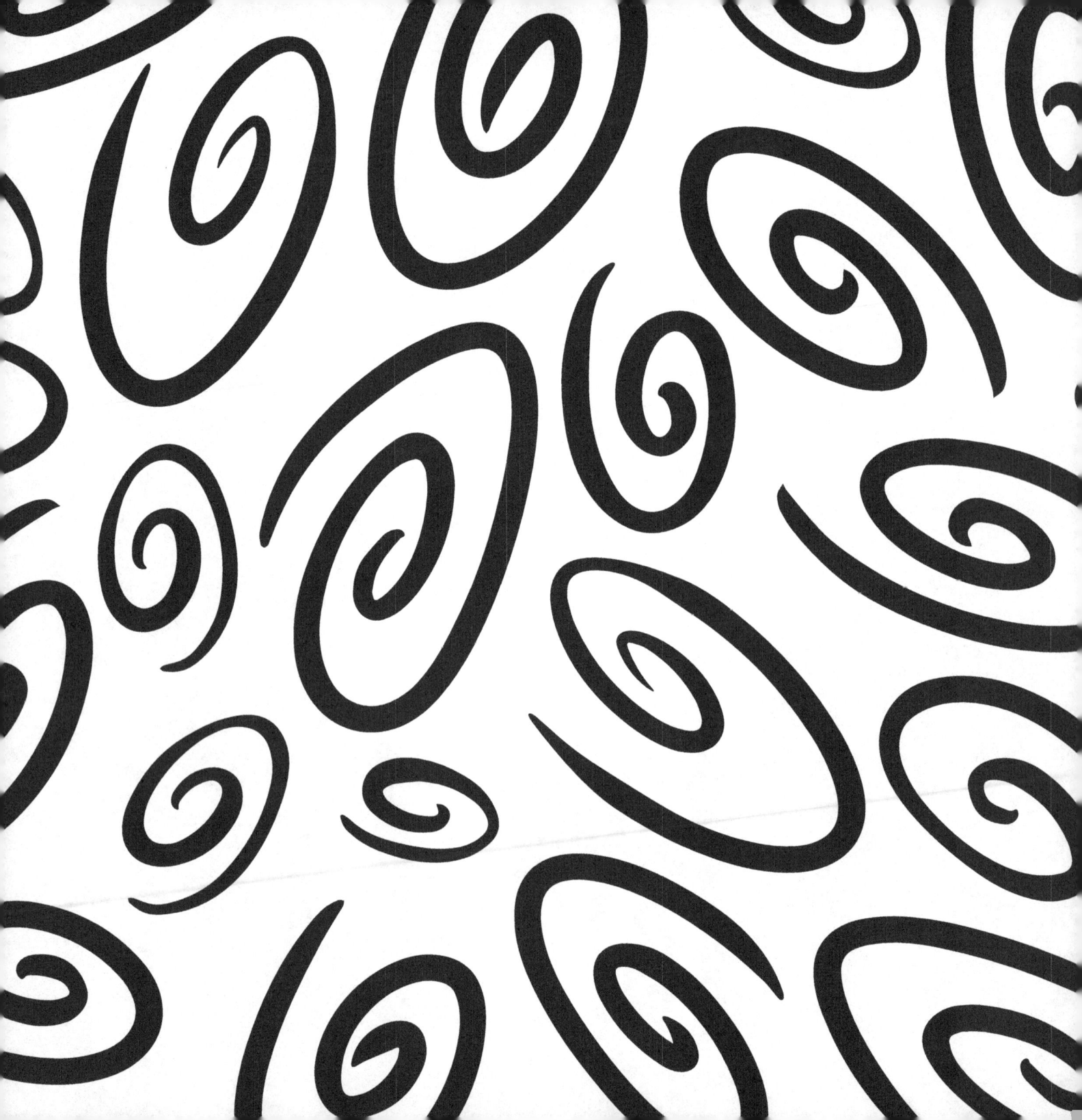

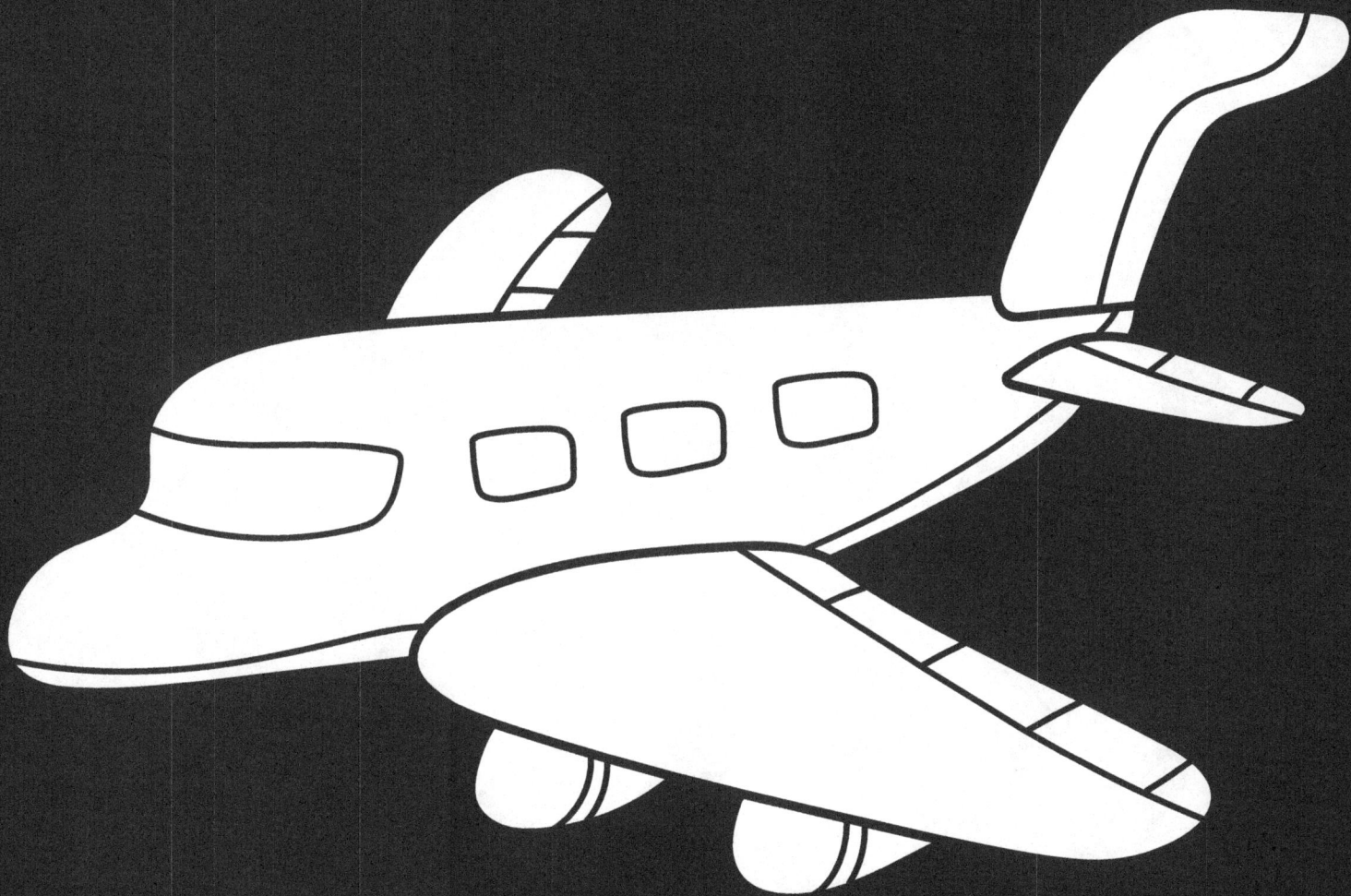

PLANE

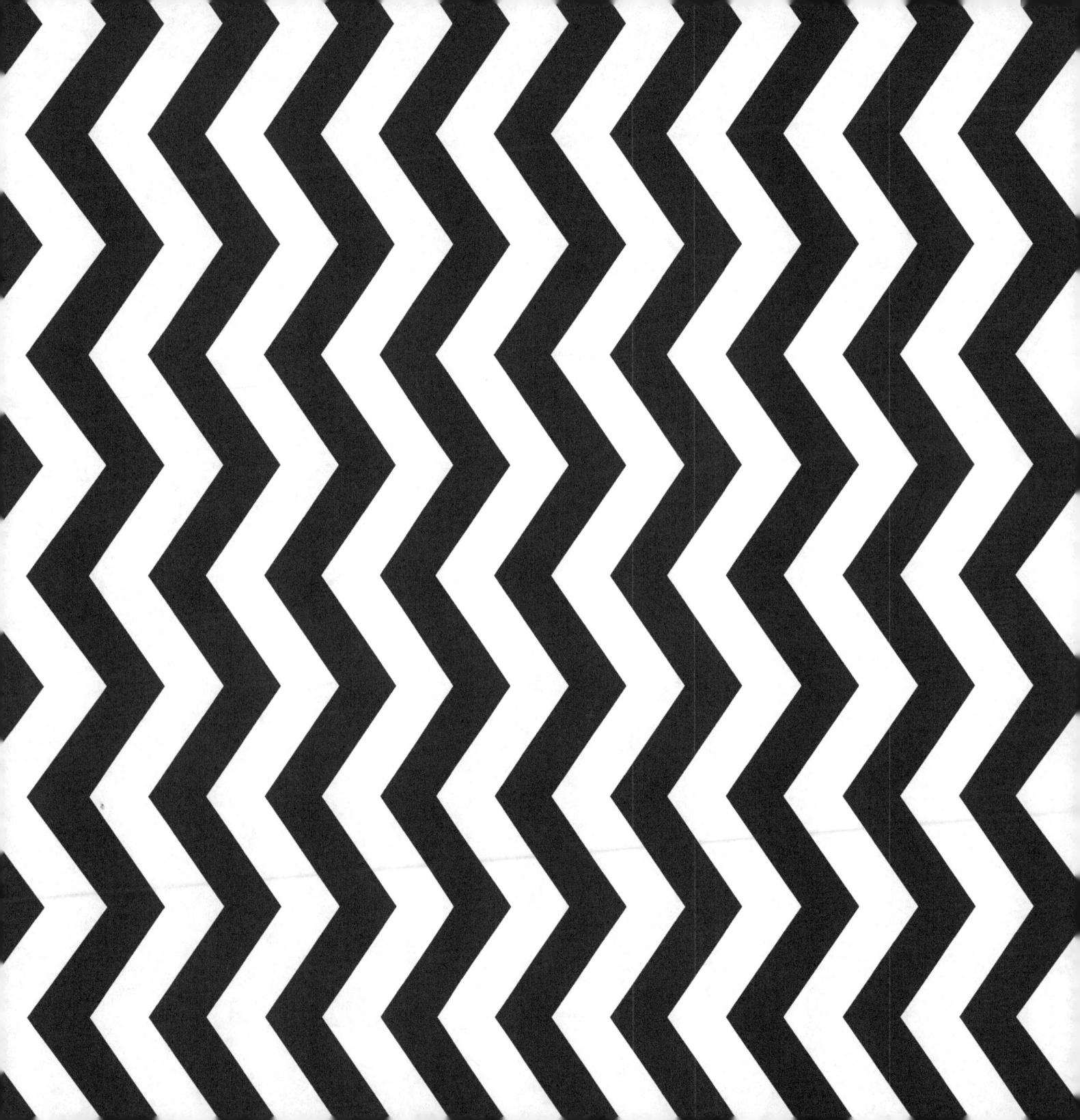

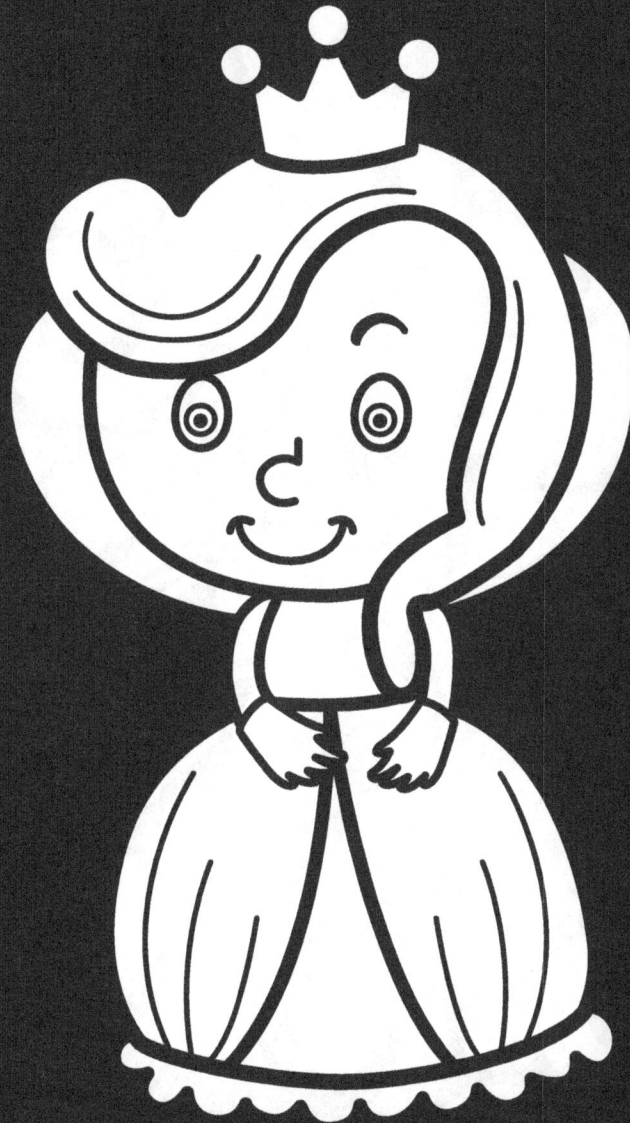

QUEEN

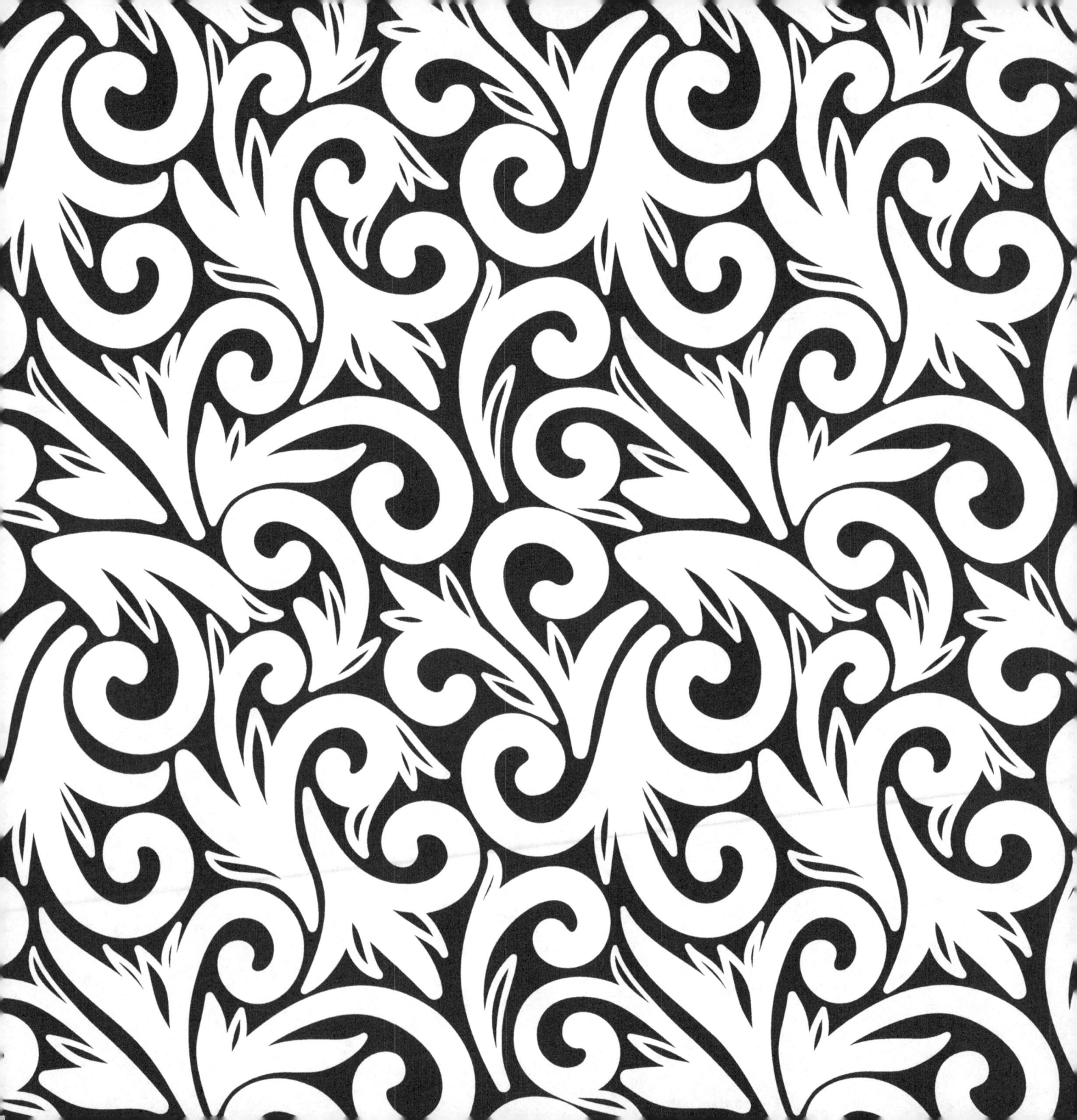

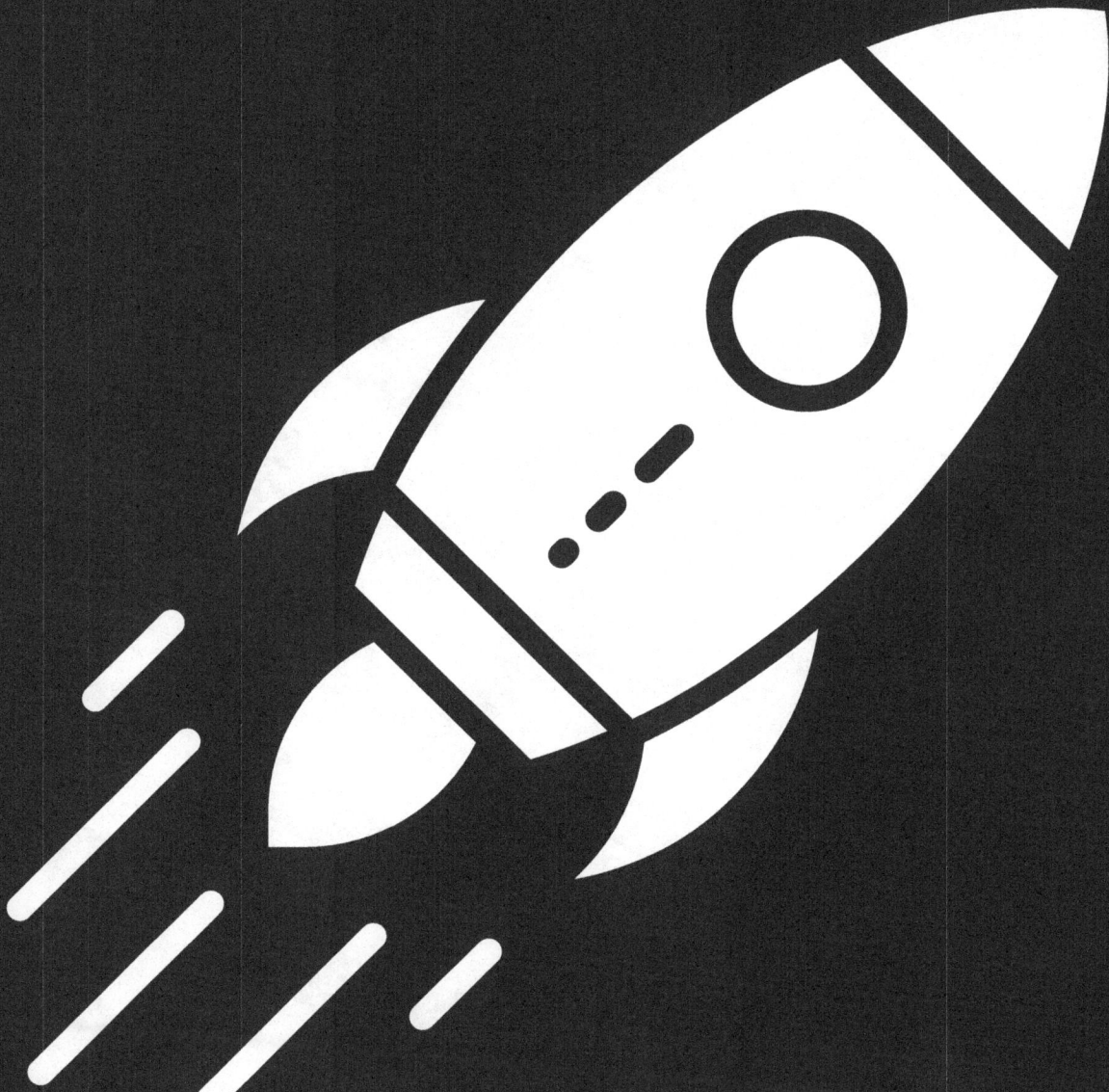

ROCKET

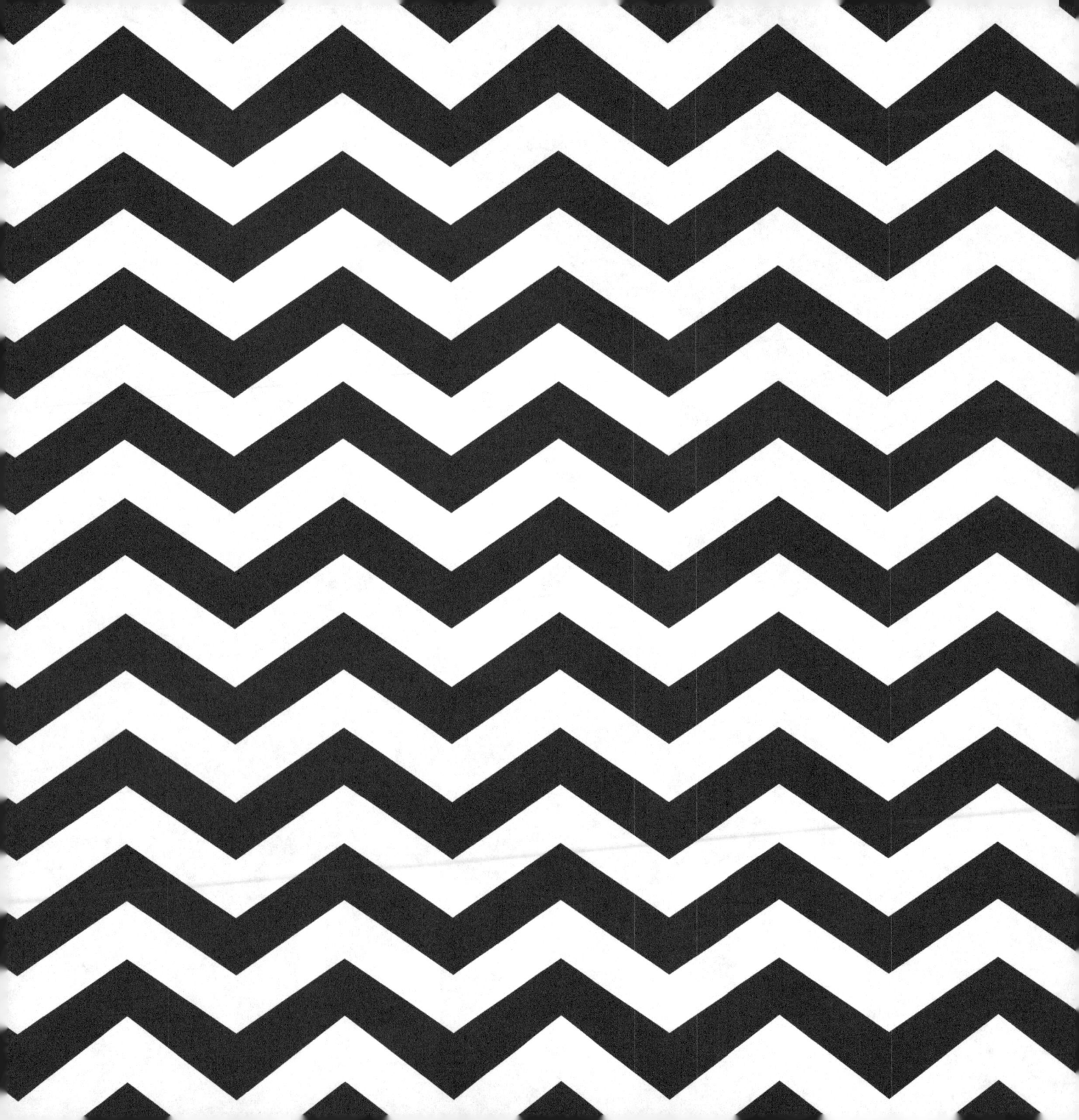

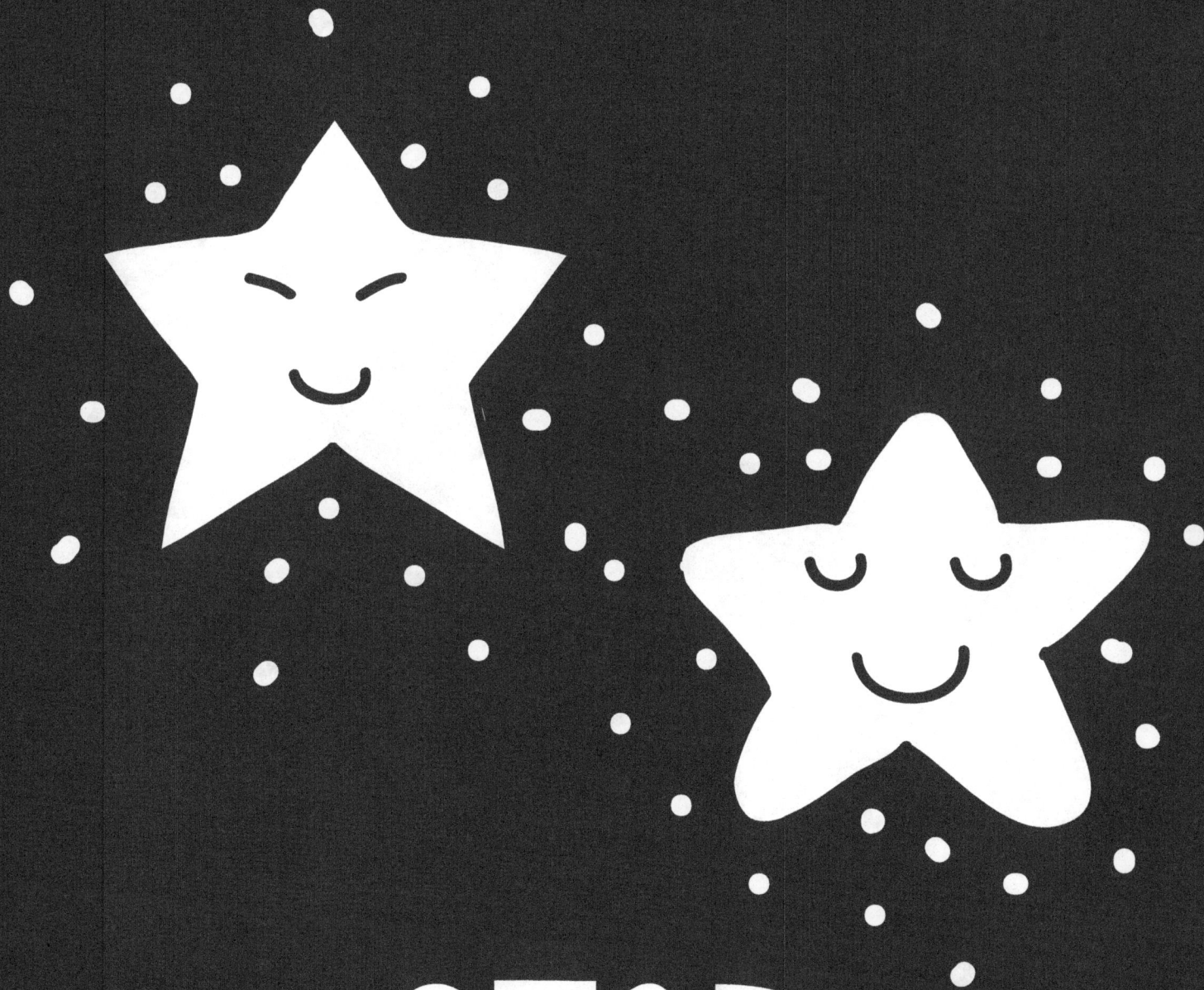

STAR

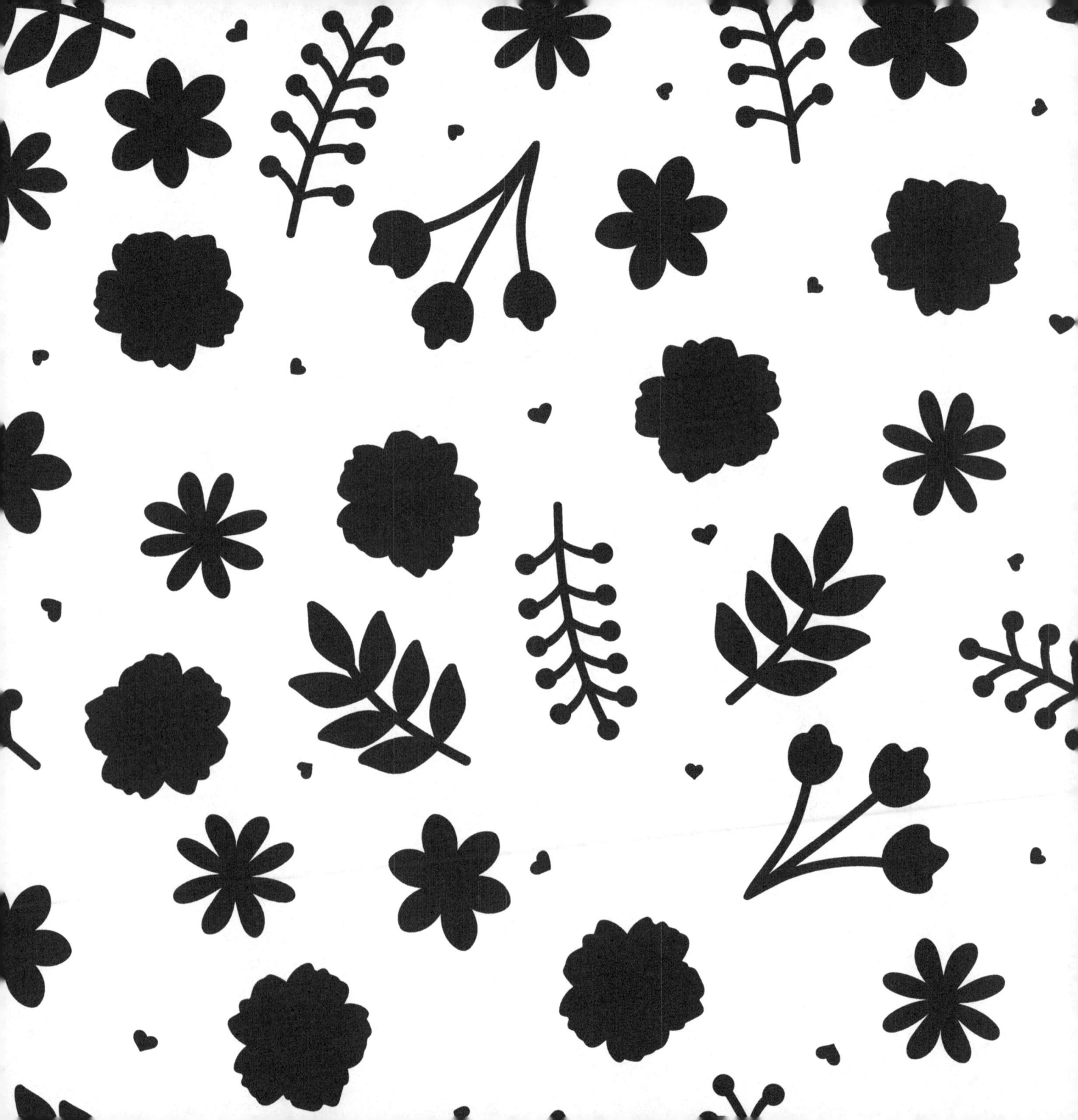

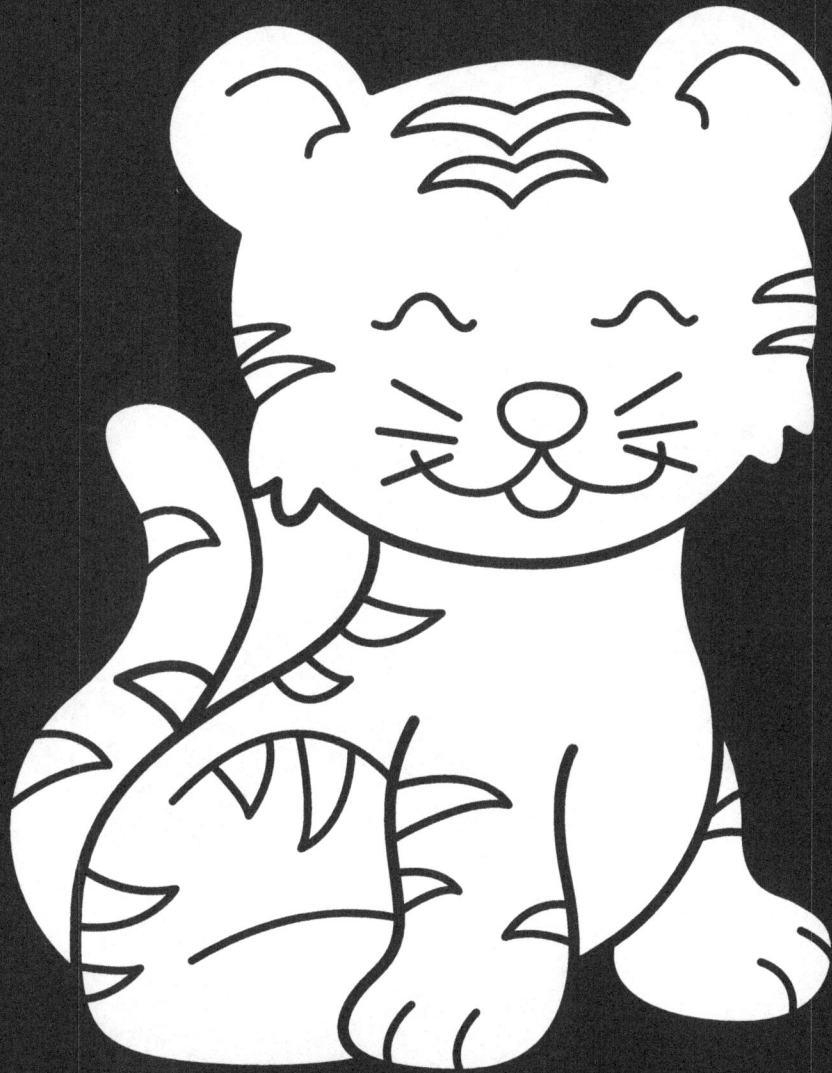

TIGER

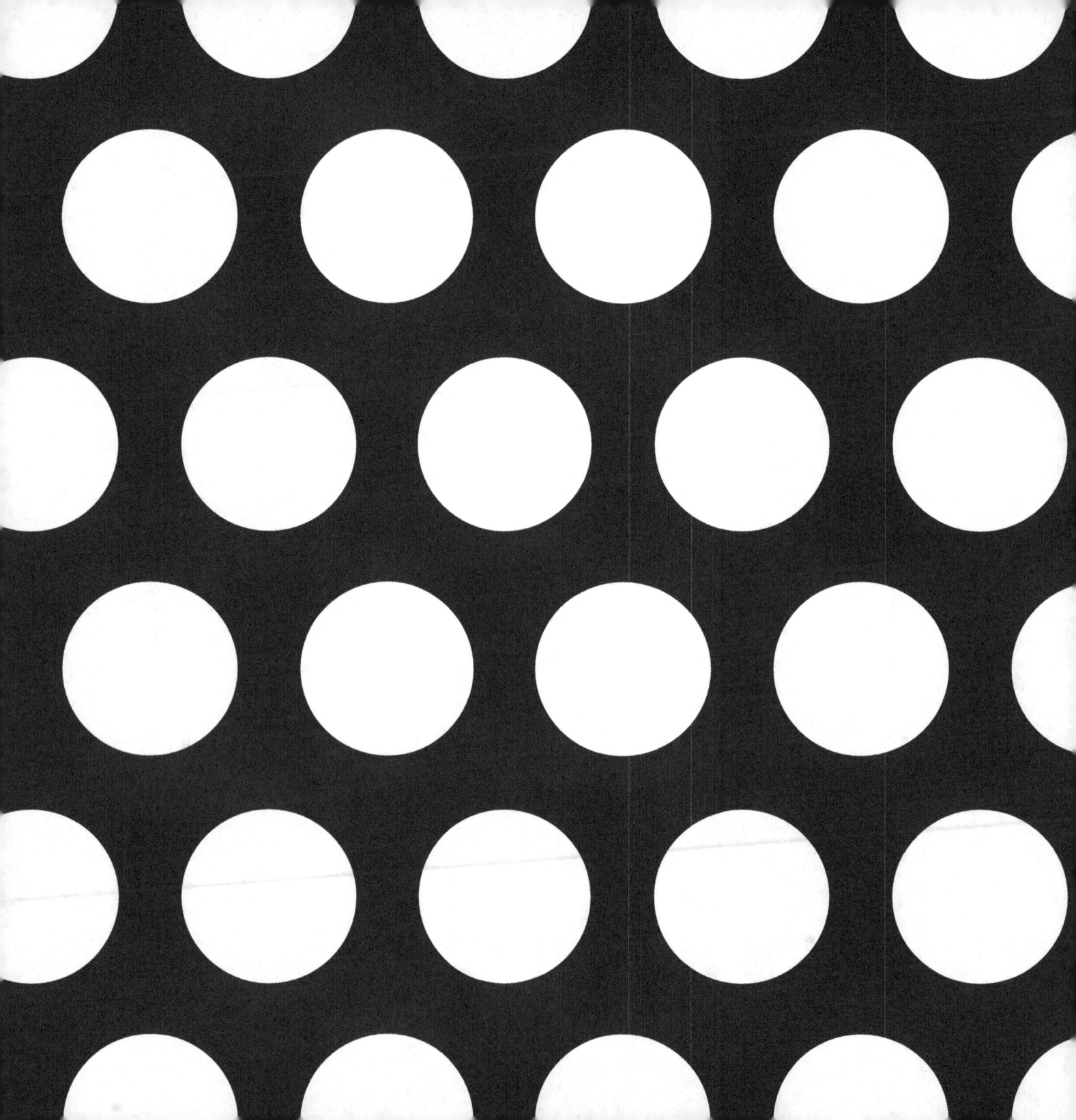

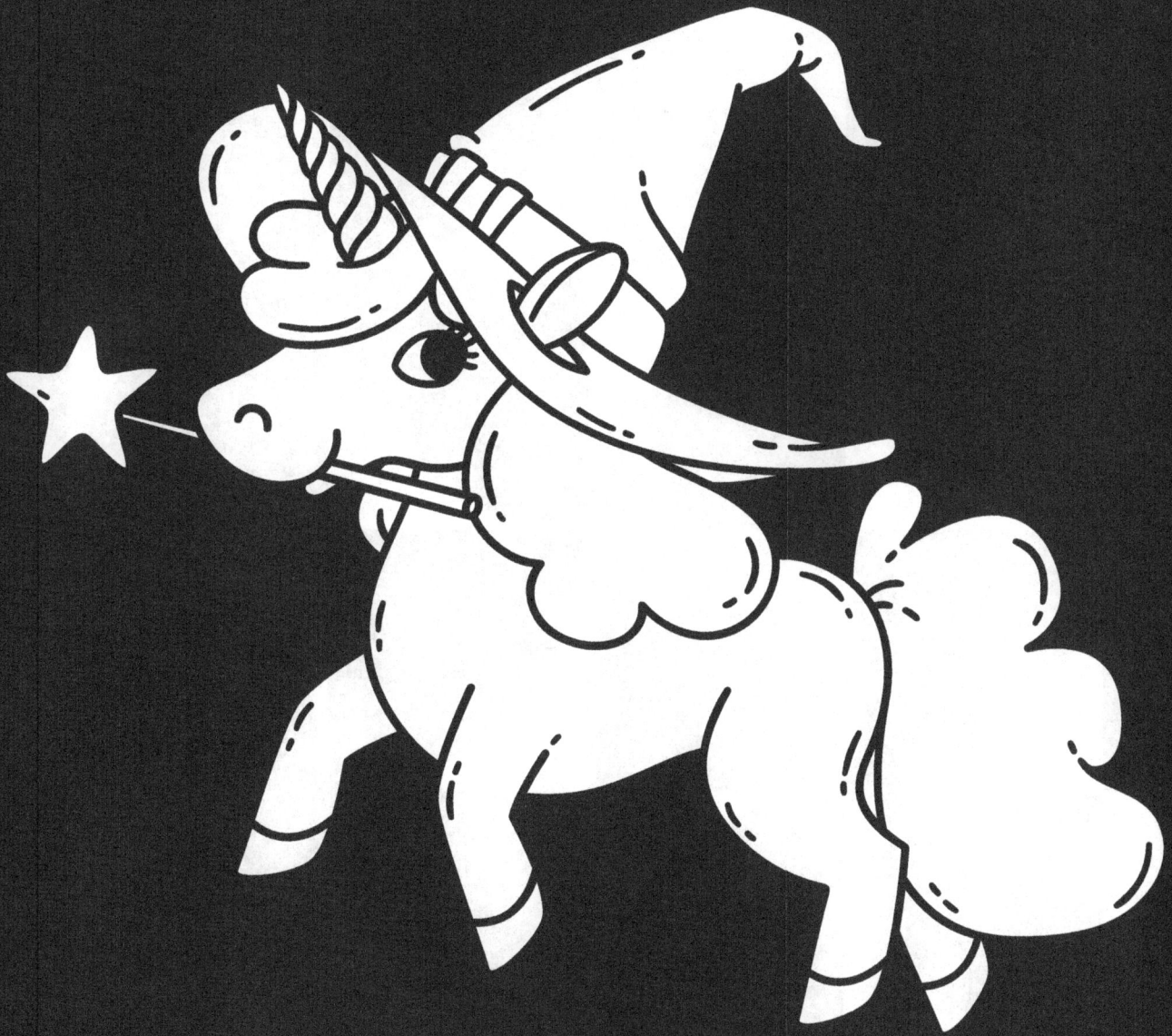

UNICORN

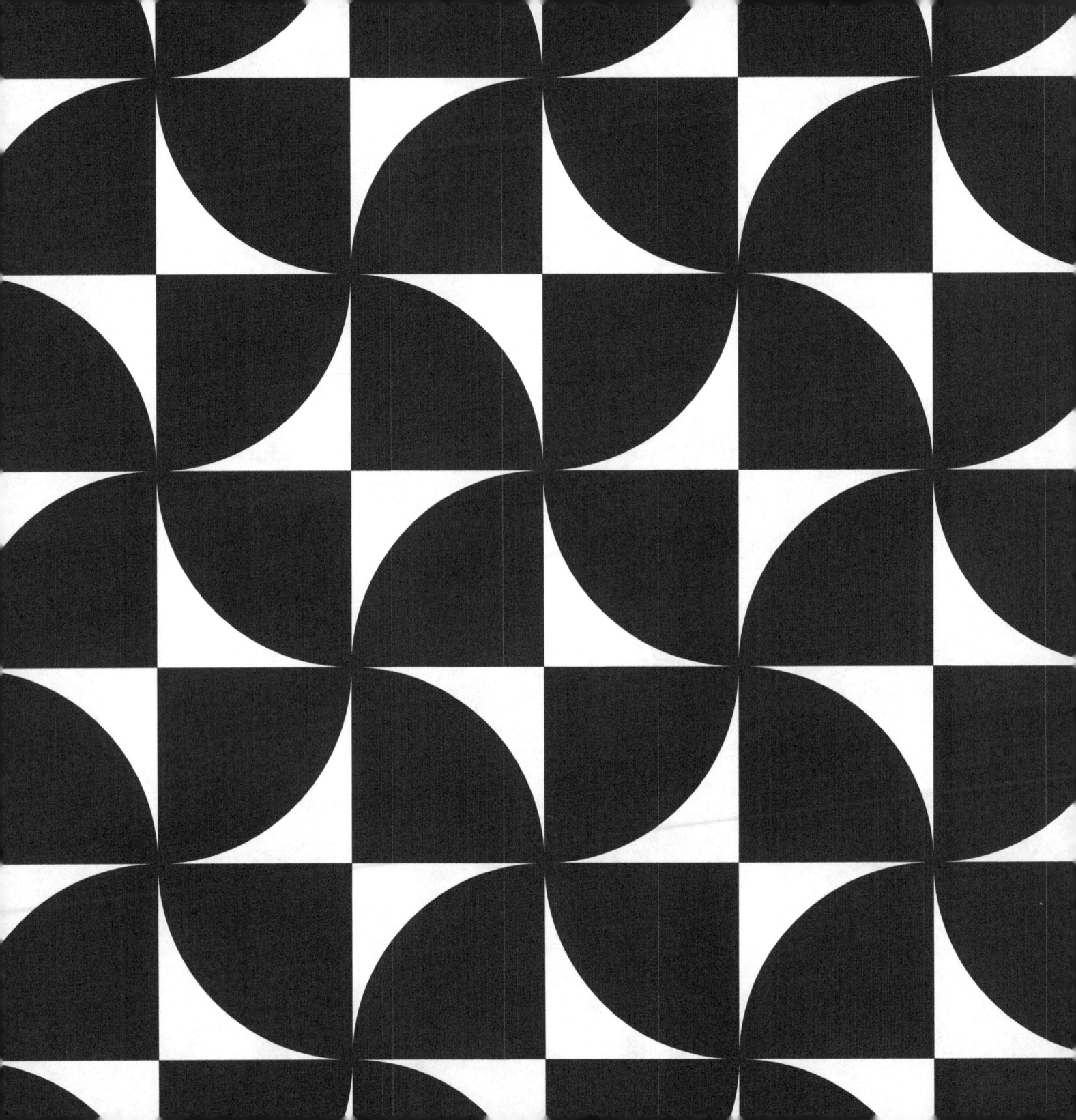

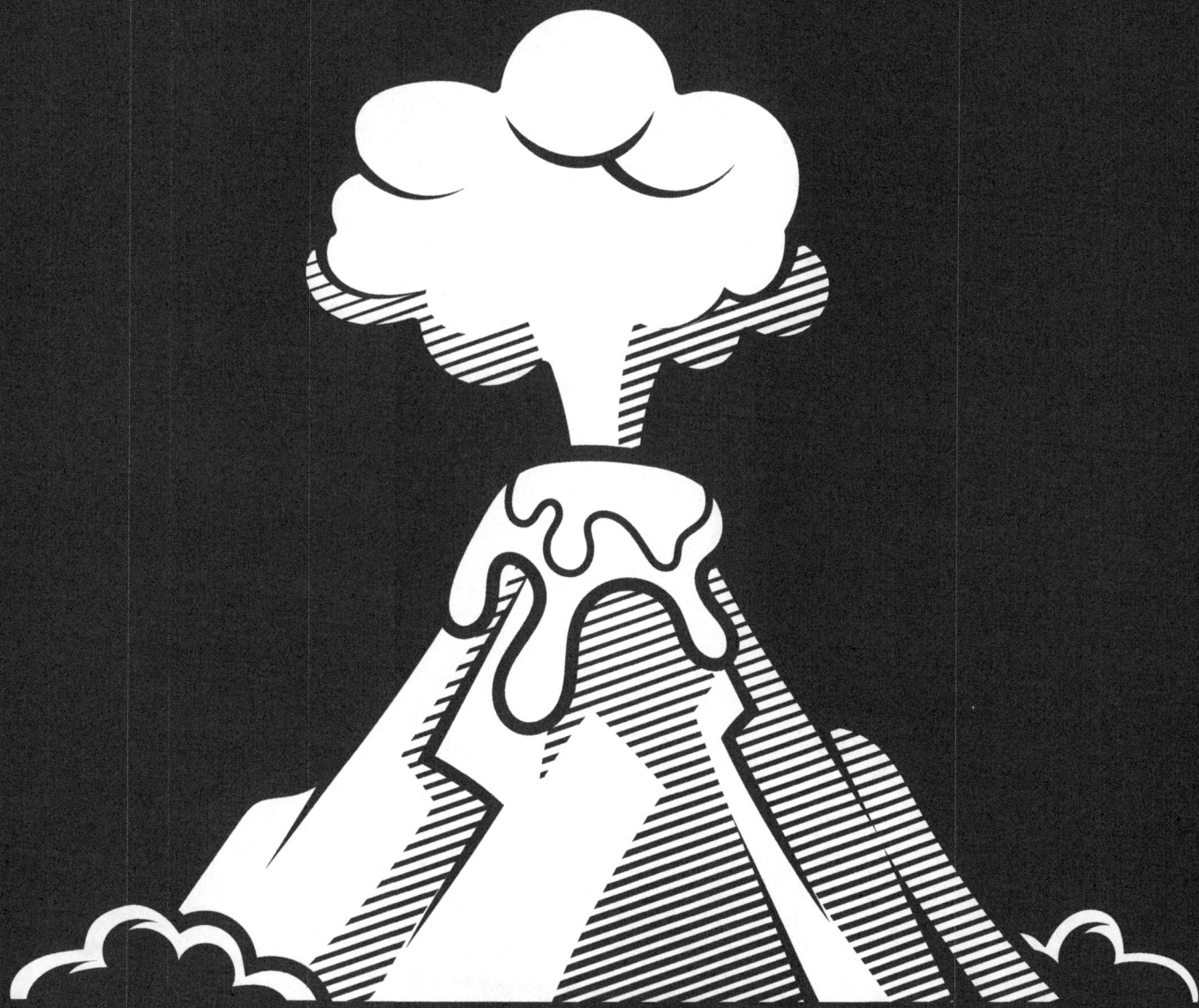

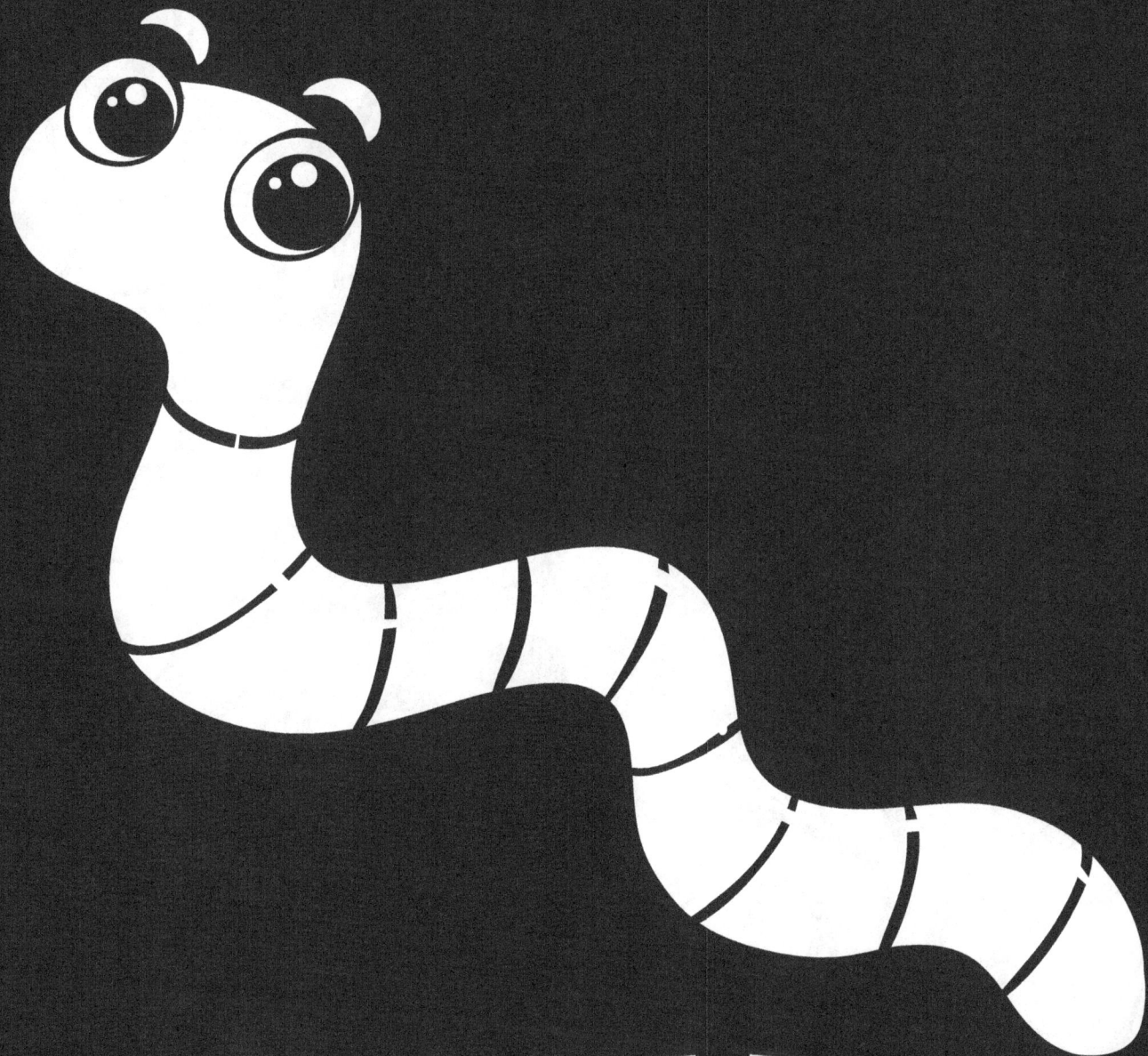

WORM

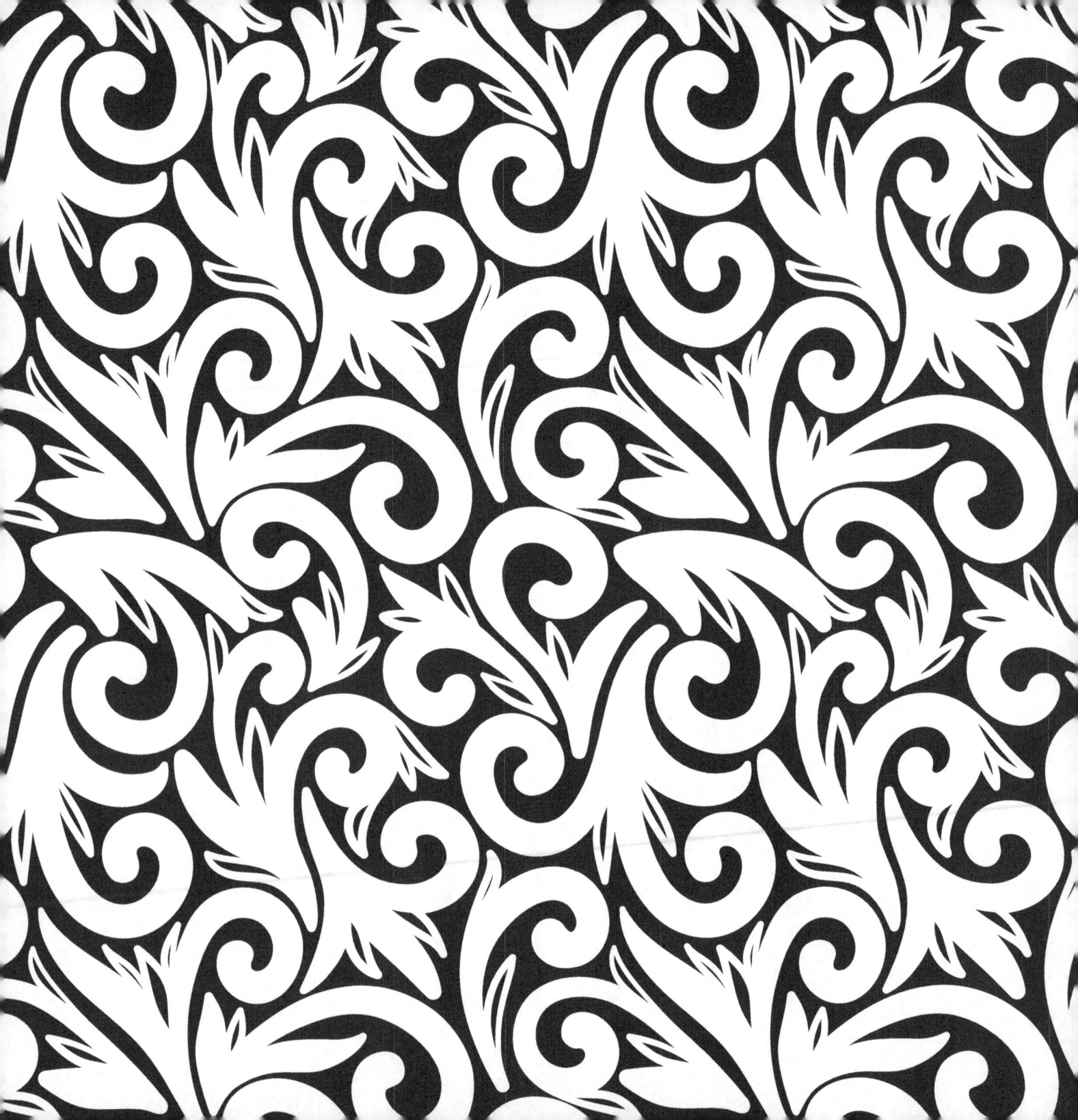

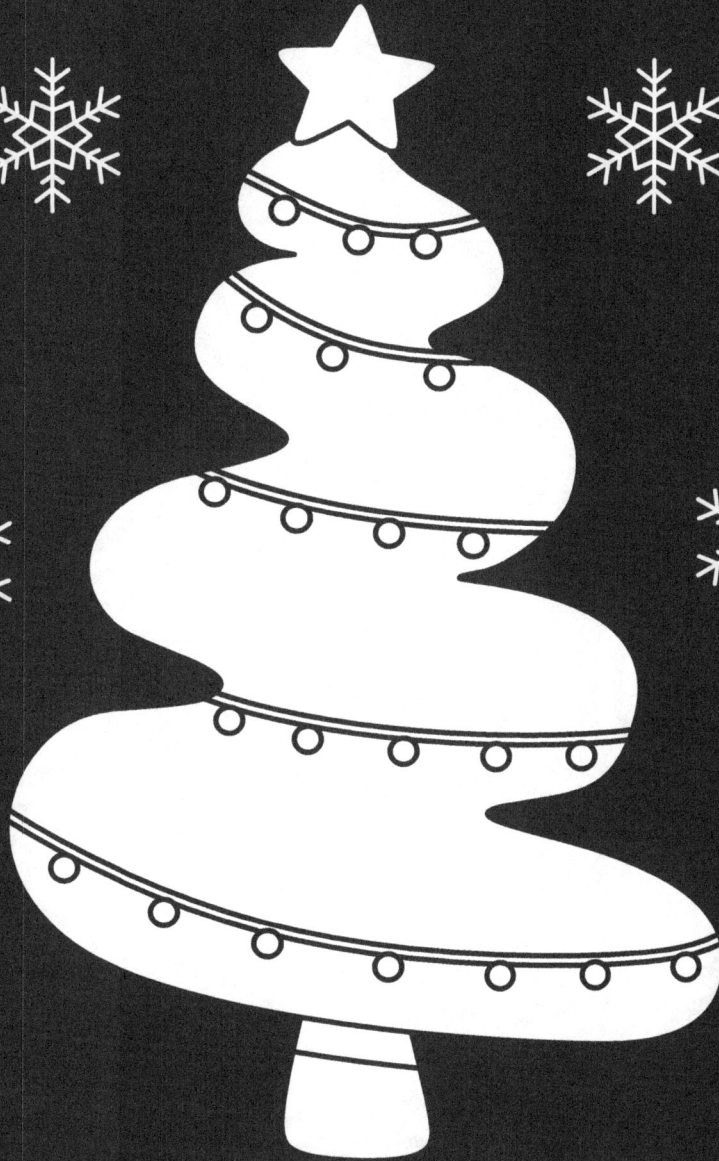

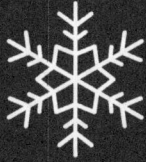

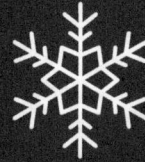

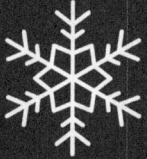

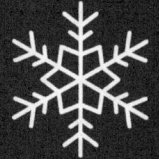

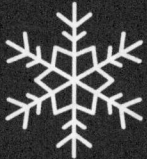

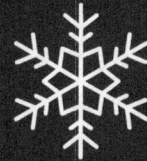

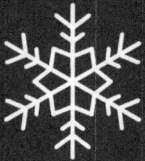

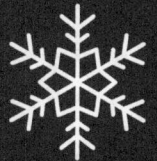

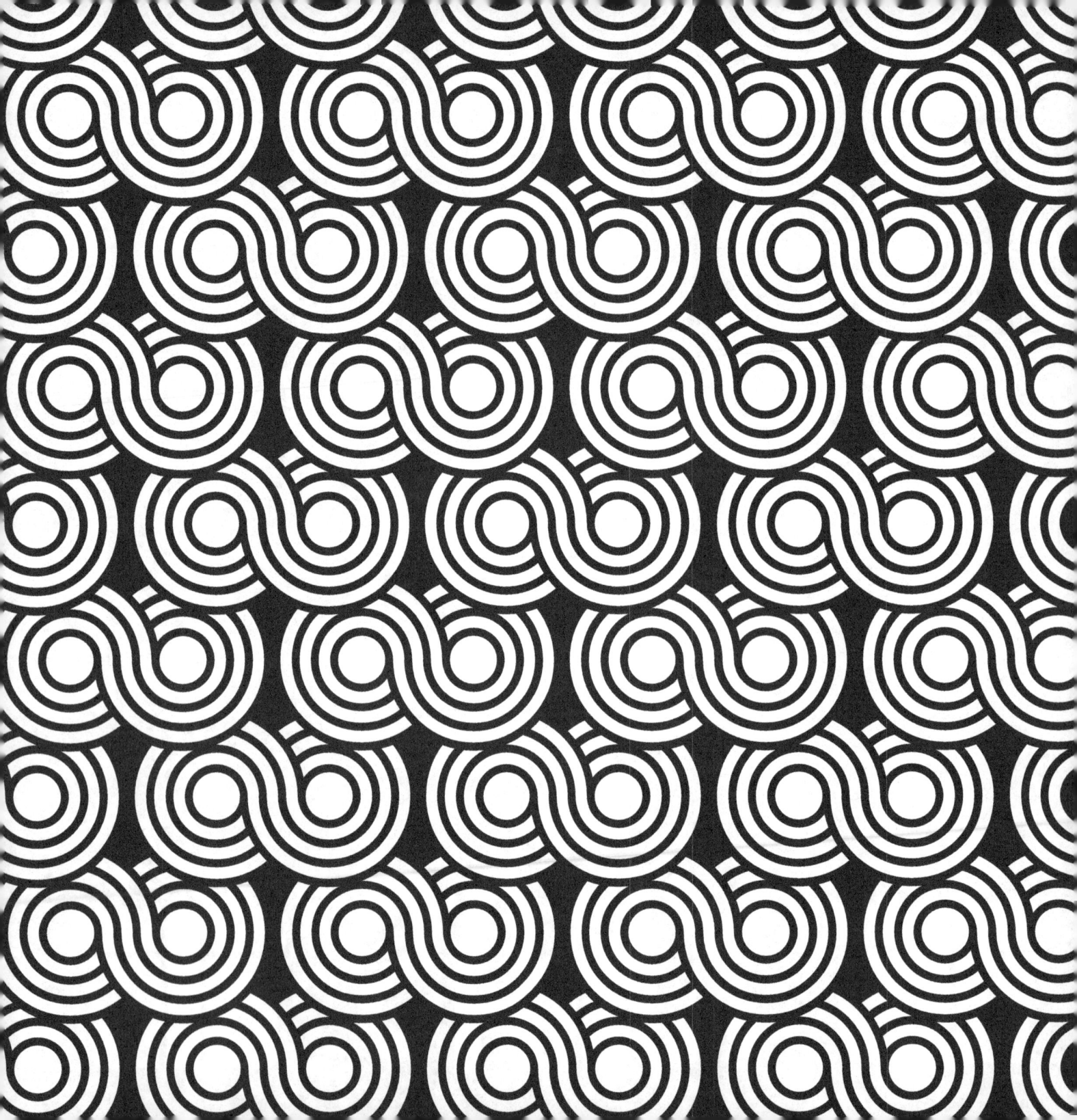

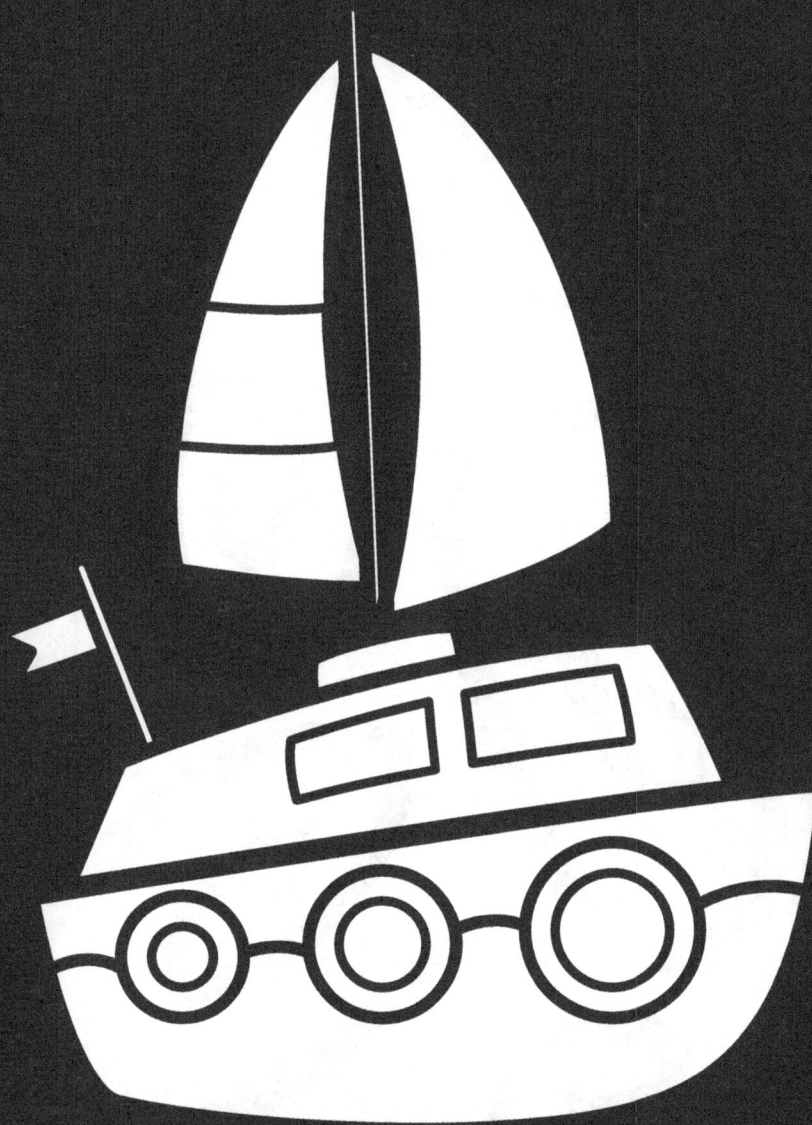

YACHT

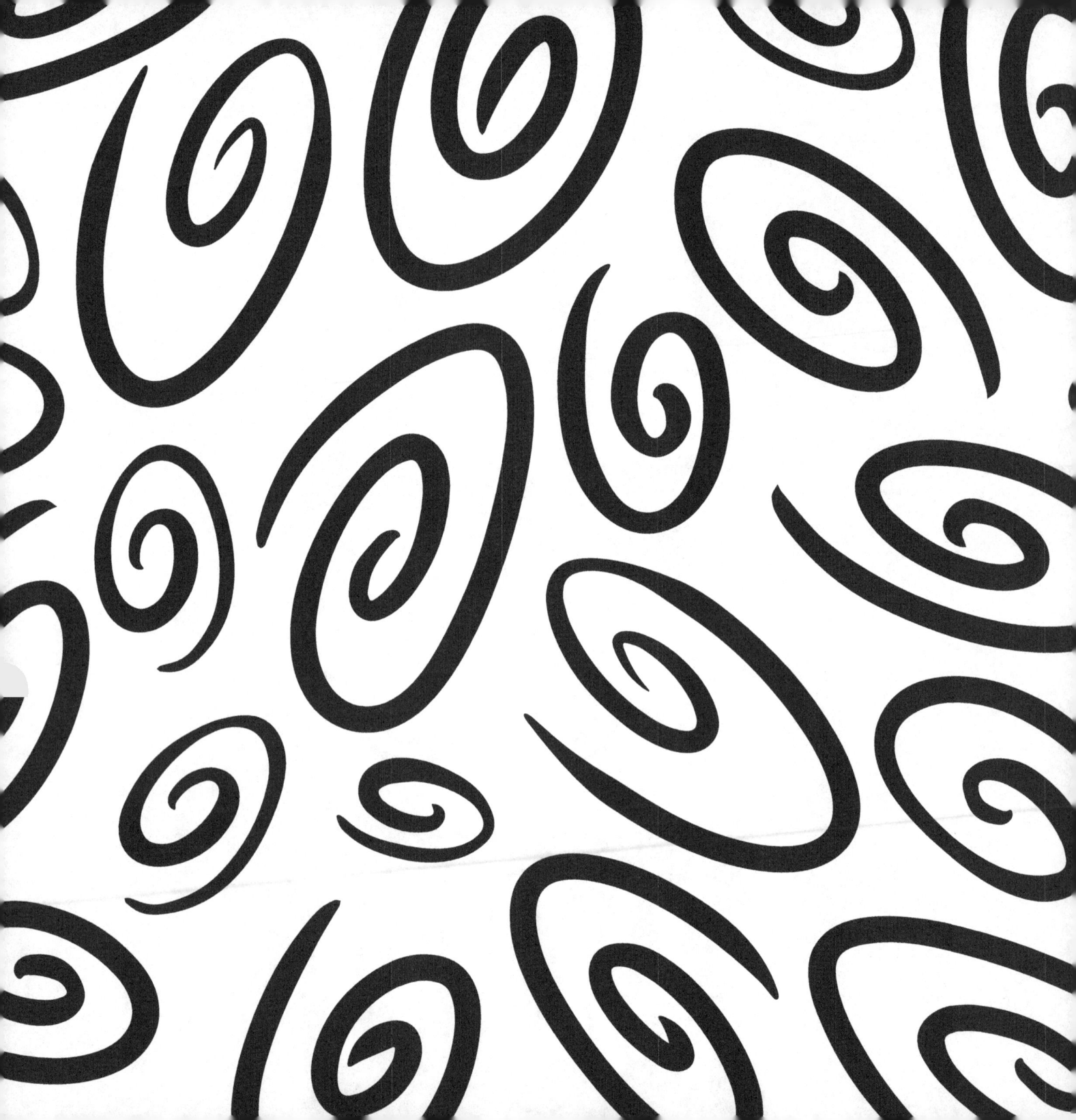

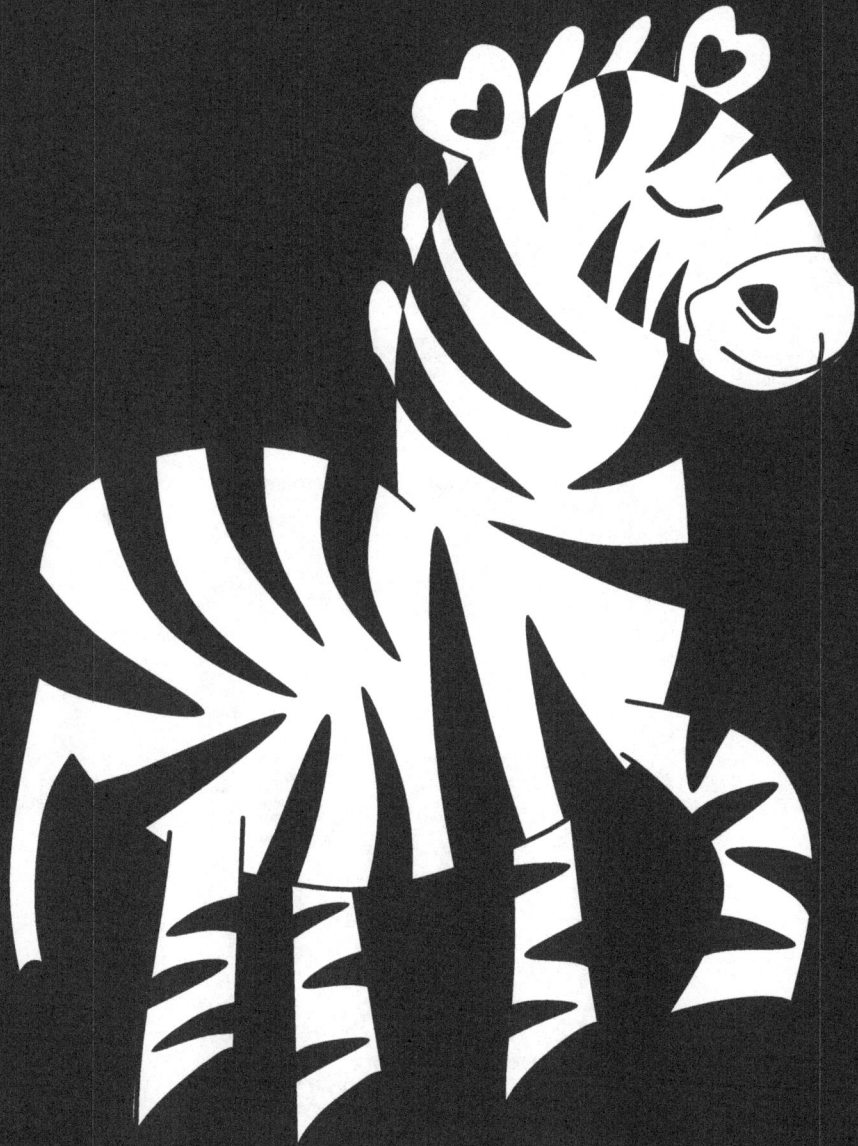

ZEBRA

GO FOR IT!

Made in the USA
Las Vegas, NV
04 April 2025